How to go from

# Employee to
# ENTREPRENEUR

**Find** your passion >>> **Start** a small business >>>
**Create** your own wealth >>>**Make** a difference

(This book is part of the *'Put Your Signature on Life'* series)

Published by PYSOL Press
2016

Published by PYSOL Press
1st Floor
3, Market Place
The Broadway
Bexleyheath
DA6 7DU

ISBN 978-1-5262-0398-4
Copyright © 2016 Bebe Clement
First published 2016

# DISCLAIMER

# DEDICATION

For Daddy.

# ACKNOWLEDGEMENTS

I would like to thank everyone who had an input into this book.

My heavenly Father, the 'giver of the gifts'. Thank you for the abundance you gave me!

My dad, who taught me to dream big, work hard and give my very best. Thank you, daddy, for all that I had the privilege of learning from you. I just wish you could have been here to see this.

To Ethel Harrad, my 'mum', for teaching me to read and write.

My dearest husband, my best friend, Seyi Clement: Baby, thanks for all the encouragement, support, love, input and subtle badgering to get the book finished.

My best friend Sandra Ramsay-Nicol, whose belief in me defies logic and who insisted that I sign up with Richard to ensure I get it finished!

My colleague and friend Dr Remi Banjoko for his input. Likewise my faithful friend and mentor, Kayode Olatuyi, I appreciate you more than I can say.

Richard McMunn, who is a living advert for this book!

My co-editors, Toyin Onabowu and Margaret Hunter, whose advice, input and suggestions made this a much better book than it would have been.

Ladi Sanni, whose first words whenever he sees me are 'When are you going to finish that book?' For your advice, guidance and support, I say thanks.

And to my 'miracle' sons, Enitan and Toyosi, thanks for coming!

# CONTENTS

The day that changed my life forever ........................................... 9

Do you want the bad news or the bad news? ........................... 13

And just when you thought it couldn't get any worse... ........... 31

Consumer price index ............................................................... 35

Scared, but prepared ................................................................ 39

The small business as an income stream ................................ 41

Who wants to be an entrepreneur (and why)? ......................... 49

Businesses don't plan to fail, they just fail to plan! ................... 53

What kind of business structure should I have? ....................... 75

A job is a place to learn (not just earn!) .................................... 81

Making the transition ................................................................. 93

15 tips for running a successful business ................................. 99

# FOREWORD

## By award-winning entrepreneur Richard McMunn

I am proud to have been invited to write this foreword for Bebe Clement, a business entrepreneur whose work I admire immensely. Bebe's organisational and entrepreneurial skills have made her what she is today – a highly successful businesswoman, who prides herself on her ability to passionately help employees make the transition from employee to business owner.

What I particularly like and admire about Bebe's own personal journey is that she has made the transition herself despite many setbacks along the way. Bebe's book explains how any employee can break out of their employment and become a successful business owner. Having taken the transition from employee to business owner myself, much of what Bebe teaches within this book resonates strongly with my own personal experiences.

The road from employee to business owner is one that more and more people are choosing to take, and this book is a must-have resource for anyone considering taking this path. The content will serve to accelerate your learning and give you the confidence needed to start the transitional steps required to achieve your own business and financial goals.

In a nutshell, if you are someone who feels trapped in your employment, or if you feel that your skills are not being used to their full potential, this book is for you.

*Richard McMunn*

# INTRODUCTION

## *The day that changed my life forever*

It was rush hour and I was on my way home from work.

It was a very hot summer's day and, the tube station was packed as always. I hate tube stations during the hot weather with everyone sweating.

The day before, with passengers packed into the carriage like a tin of sardines, I had spent most of the journey with my head trapped under the armpit of a sweaty man who looked and was dressed like a heavyweight wrestler, and whose armpits smelled like prawns that had gone off! As on most days, I was tired and not looking forward to the mad dash to the nursery to pick up my two sons before the six o'clock deadline, after which the nursery would start charging me £5 for every 15 minutes I was late.

As I came round the corner of the station onto a near empty platform, I realised that I had just missed a train. And then it happened...

Right in front of me, on a large poster, was an elderly couple sitting in their living room. The decor of the room was dated, like it was probably from the seventies, with roses on the carpet and flowered wallpaper. The room itself was clean but sparsely furnished. You got the impression that money was clearly not in abundance.

The couple were dressed in their dressing gowns and slippers, watching a small, old-fashioned TV with an aerial placed in the middle. In the caption, the husband was asking his wife, 'Do you remember that time when we *almost* went on holiday?'

As I read those words, I had one of those moments you see in the movies when the picture or whatever the actor is looking at becomes really big and up close. Everyone else on that platform suddenly disappeared from my view. I might as well have been standing there alone. I started having an anxiety attack and sweat began trickling down my face and back; suddenly I couldn't breathe.

Then I heard a voice (I'm a Christian, so I'll call it the voice of the Holy Spirit): *'Bebe! If you don't do something about your financial situation, this is going to be you in a few years' time, looking back with regret and trying to reach for non-existent memories to keep you warm in your old age.'*

What made it even stranger was that I wasn't poor or even unemployed. In fact, I was an employment law adviser for a trade union. I wasn't wealthy, but my husband, who is a solicitor and I were well able to meet our financial obligations. We were doing 'OK'.

But somehow, in that moment, it was impressed upon me that I had to make a decision, **right there and then**, to change my financial situation. Don't ask me how, but I knew that if I waited till the next day, or indeed until I left the station, to make that decision, it would be too late. So, I said a silent prayer of thanks and made a promise that I would indeed change my life.

I immediately set to work to set up my own company, a consultancy providing bespoke employment law and HR advice to small businesses and employees, which I ran from one of my bedrooms (and still do).

Very soon, the income from the company matched and then doubled my salary, which was great because, a few months later, my two-year-old son (who was not yet talking and had been exhibiting some really bizarre behaviour) was diagnosed as being severely autistic, and I had to give up my job to take care of him.

# CHAPTER 1

*Do you want
the bad news or
the bad news?*

Have you ever watched archers shooting at targets? If so, you will notice that they don't just come up to the stand and take their shot. Instead, the first thing they do is pull the bow back, before taking aim and finally, they shoot. Why don't they just shoot? Because that pullback helps improve aim and greatly increases the likelihood of hitting the desired target.

If you don't mind, I'd like to take the same approach with this book. So, before we start talking about your job and business, I'm going to pull back and talk a little bit about capitalism. Why? Because a basic understanding of capitalism is vital to your financial success. It provides the **why** behind your setting up a business, and if you understand why, as a 21st-century employee, you **must** set up a business or establish other income streams, you're more likely to commit to the **how** – or the process – and thus significantly improve your chances of success in business. A large majority of business success is down to **mindset**, and, hopefully, this part of the book will help you establish the right one.

Also, any house is only as good as the foundation you build it on, and one of the main reasons why people do not do well financially and have to remain as employees all their lives, is because they have a poor foundation when it comes to money matters and do not understand the nature of the economic environment in which they are operating.

Sadly, those in charge of the education system do not deem it necessary to equip us in this area. Rather, I remember being taught the importance of being able to correctly dissect a toad. Guess how many times I've had to dissect a toad since leaving school?

Most people don't understand the rules of the game (and I assure you, it is a game) that they have to play to become financially successful and independent.

Imagine someone playing a game when they don't understand the rules. Would you agree that, even though their failure is not guaranteed, their chances of winning are greatly diminished? Of course they are, so this bit is important and you need to **pay attention, please**.

# What is capitalism?

Capitalism is a socioeconomic **system** whereby the factors of production (i.e. the ingredients needed to keep an economy going) – land, labour and capital – are **controlled** and **privately owned** by a very small group of people.

> The fuel for a capitalist economy is greed, and it exists purely to make profit.

Remember, a capitalist society does not exist to improve the state of the common people. (That's you and me, by the way.)

In a capitalist system there are three main types of people:

1. **The capitalists** – who are smart and own capital, property, land, shares, bonds, businesses and numerous other investments.

2. **The middle class** – mostly professionals such as doctors, lawyers, engineers, managers and senior civil servants, who are usually dependent on a salary, but who are made to believe that, since they are climbing up the economic ladder, surely they must be making progress.

3. **The working class** – those in lower paid, often unskilled jobs, such as bricklayers, cleaners and street cleaners.

Rich Hall, an American comedian, says: "When you go to work in the morning, if your name is on the building—you're rich, if your name is on your desk—you're middle class, and if your name is on your shirt—you're poor!"[1]

For the purposes of this book, I'm going to lump the last two groups together because, in my view, the middle class (to which I belong) are just the glorified working class. They are in the same sinking ship! Their dependence on a salary will leave them 'Just Over Broke' or 'JOB'. (See what I did there?) It doesn't matter how much you earn, because your appetites tend to increase in proportion to your salary. If, for example, your salary goes from 30–50k, you will discover that you suddenly want a new car, or a larger house in a better neighbourhood, and once you've purchased them, **in real terms**, you are right back where you started.

Now, you will have noticed that some of the words in the above definitions of capitalism are in bold letters; that's because they are very important. So important is their understanding to your financial success that I am going to break them down for you.

## Capitalism is a system

By my definition, a system is something that has intelligent design behind it with a particular outcome in mind. So, what is the outcome in mind where a capitalist system is concerned?

The most important one for the working class is that the system is designed so that **the working class forever remain working class**. People in this category are the fodder for making money, and without us the whole system collapses. The system is designed so that you are paid just enough money to keep you walking through that door every morning; in other words, just enough to survive but not thrive, or just enough to live, but not have a life.

When you get your salary at the end of each month and find, a few days later, that you have no money left, that is not an accident. **It is designed to happen that way.** It's not even because you are living beyond your means (although many of us are) – it's all part of the system.

Another way the system works is to ensure that any money the working class get from it by way of salary **will be put back into the system**.

Just when you've finished paying the mortgage, the car insurance is due, and when you've paid that, the TV licence is due, and then you have to service the boiler… Sound familiar? But more on that later.

There is a more subtle, but extremely effective way that the capitalists control the finances of the working class. Here's an example:

Would you agree that it's practically impossible to live in the western world without insurance? There's car insurance, home contents insurance, landlord's insurance, health insurance, life insurance… the list is endless.

Here's a question for you. Do you or anybody you know **own** shares in an insurance company? I doubt it. Who do you think owns insurance companies? Yes, capitalists. Now you're getting it!

Let's take another look. Out of an already insufficient income, the working class are **forced** (with the backing of the law), to make a wide range of financial purchases in an industry that they have little or no financial stake in, or reward from. Rather, that reward goes to those who **own** shares in that industry, the capitalists.

Now, I am not saying that the requirement for insurance is a bad thing in itself, but even where people have paid into that system for years, getting what they are owed when the time comes can prove an uphill task.

In the summer of 2007, Hull, a town in East Yorkshire, England, was heavily hit by floods. Paul Hendy, who was working with families on insurance issues for Hull City Council following the floods, and is a leading expert in the field, was quoted in *The Guardian* on 9th December 2007 as saying:

*The way insurance companies have dealt with their customers in the aftermath of the summer floods is nothing short of disgusting.*

He went on to state that some of the country's biggest insurers were the worst offenders when it came to carrying out work on flood-hit houses.

One of the couples interviewed, Rod and Jo McDonagh, from Muchelney, were flooded for 10 weeks, with a repair bill totalling £130,000. Since then, their insurance costs have risen from £5,000 to £9,000.

However, the article ended with this message of hope:

*A new scheme called **Flood Re** will be introduced in 2015 which should ensure flood insurance is widely affordable and available.*[2]

Source: Association of British Insurers

Sadly, it was not to be.

On 2nd January 2016 the Mail on Sunday published a story by Martin Delgado & Nigel Bunyan highlighting the plight of flood victims who were optimistically waiting for Flood Re to commence, three years after it had been promised.

**First flooded, then fleeced: Victims forced to pay out thousands despite being promised £180 million in Government insurance three years ago**

*Thousands of flood victims whose homes and businesses were ravaged in the storms are facing financial ruin because a Government-backed scheme giving them the legal right to affordable insurance has been delayed.*

*The needless hold-ups have heaped more misery on families whose lives have been devastated by the torrential downpours. They now face horrendous repair bills they cannot pay.*

*A* Mail on Sunday *investigation has revealed that the scheme, called Flood Re, was first mooted in 2012 and should have been launched last July, but because of the Government and the insurance industry dragging their feet it was called off twice and now will not be in place until April.*[3]

My crystal ball tells me they will be waiting a long time, because the capitalists will fight with everything they can to protect their wealth and ensure that the working class don't get our grubby little hands on it!

# Ownership

You are going to hear me talk a lot about ownership. Why is ownership so important? Because, in a capitalist society, **ownership translates into profit for the owner**.

Politicians would have us believe that the wealth of this nation belongs to every Tom, Raj and Olu (how's that for political correctness?) and that, if we work hard enough, that wealth is up for grabs. **We must not buy into this, because it is simply not true.**

The wealth of this nation belongs to those who **own**, period – **own** properties, **own** land, **own** businesses, **own** investments, **own** shares, and so on.

In my view, apart from winning the lottery, the only way to get a slice of the nation's financial cake is to make sure you have numerous income streams, because your salary will only ever award you crumbs.

For more information on my Wealth Creation Seminars, visit www.bebeclement.com/training or drop me an email at bebe@bebeclement.com.

## Whoever controls your time controls you!

Now, a word of warning. You may not like what I'm about to say here, but I'm hoping that grasping this concept will make you angry enough to actually **do something** about your situation. OK, here goes.

If you are in a job (either full-time or part-time), and you have **no other source of income** other than your salary, then you are the 'labour' in the above definition of capitalism and you are **controlled** and pretty much **owned** by the capitalists.

When I say this during my business and wealth creation seminars, I sometimes see frowns and looks of indignation on delegates' faces – until I show them the evidence. My background is in law so I'm really big on evidence. So let's examine it shall we?

What do you think is your greatest resource in life? The majority of working class people think it's money, which is why they spend most of their lives exchanging their time for money by way of a salary.

It's not.

## Time is your greatest resource in life.

Why do you think that is?

Because you can never get it back.

Where wealth in particular is concerned (and indeed in many other areas of our lives), there are certain things you must know and have done by the age of 20, certain others by the age of 30, and yet more by the age of 40, which, if you have not, barring a miracle, you will be playing 'catch-up' for the rest of your life because you are running out of time.

Therefore, if someone can say that you must be in the office by 9.00 every day; you cannot go to lunch until 12.00, and then you only have 30 minutes; you must not leave until 5.30 every day; you can only have 28 days off in the year for a holiday, and if (God forbid) you fall ill, you can only have a certain number of days off to recover from that illness before they start making your life hell… in other words, if someone can control your **time**, your greatest resource in life, in that way, then **they control you**!

Unfortunately, that is the nature of the game for most working class people, because what we exchange for our salaries is our **ability to work**, signified by our **presence** in the workplace, and presence requires a surrendering of our greatest resource – **time**. And the minute that is hampered in any way by lateness, illness, pregnancy, personal issues, family or the like, potentially we are in trouble.

Capitalists in their wisdom understand this principle perfectly; that's why they are always happy to **trade their money for time**. The working class sadly live this principle backwards; they spend most of their lives in the workplace. In other words they **trade their time for money**. If you do not understand the subtle difference between these two concepts, it will cost you dearly! You can always get back money (just ask Donald Trump), **but you can never get back time.**

Capitalists know that, in order for them to continue enjoying the life they are living, the working class must stay in their place; otherwise they will aspire to be like them. After all, there is nothing special about capitalists; they each have one head, just like you and me. But, they **make their money work hard for them**, whereas the working class **work hard for their money.**

More importantly, capitalists know that in order to realise any aspirations to be like them, you must be able to think clearly, you must be able to plan, strategize and carry out that strategy, and all that you have put in place must bear fruit. All these things take **time**. So, the best way to keep the working class in their place is to control their greatest resource – **time**.

Nobody ever says this to you of course and it's not written down anywhere, but what happens is: you wake up one day and you're 50 or 60, and you suddenly realise that, by way of financial reward, you have little or nothing to show for the past 30 years of your life, and you are facing a retirement of near poverty. Even if you are not, let's face it, by the time you retire, your best years are behind you. Why should anyone want to wait till they are 60 to have a life? In the past nine months I have sadly had to attend the funerals of two of my friends, both of whom were in their 40s. **Live now**, because tomorrow is not guaranteed!

# Ownership is everything

When I do wealth creation seminars, I actually get my delegates to say the following sentence out loud, and I'd like you to do the same now.

**In a capitalist society, ownership is everything!**

Say it again, because I need you to remember this.

**In a capitalist society, ownership is everything!**

Thank you.

The reason ownership is so important is because **ownership translates into profit**. It is this profit that capitalists use to send their children to the best schools (where A*s are the norm), while the children of the working class mainly go to the local comprehensive (where overworked, disillusioned teachers in classes filled largely with children who have very little understanding of the importance of education, and even less ambition, have been forced to replace teaching with 'crowd control'. The education system is another effective way capitalists use to ensure that the working class stay in their place from generation to generation – but that's for another book!

**Profit** also buys membership into the best social clubs, where members are on first-name terms with those in power – those who make decisions about **your** life.

It is **profit** that pays for the best professional advice to help evade and avoid paying tax and to ensure that wealth is hidden away from the tax authorities in tax havens, which protects and preserves wealth for generations to come, whereas employees' wages are taxed at source, **before** they even get paid!

It is **profit** that buys **time** – time to think, time to create, time to strategize, time to execute strategies, time to rest and time to recuperate properly after an illness.

Most importantly from my point of view, it is **profit** that buys **choices** – choices that enable people to **enjoy** (rather than just endure) life.

Think about it for a minute. Seriously, **what is life without choices?**

The importance of the choices that financial freedom affords was brought home to me recently in a very personal way.

My younger son applied to three secondary schools, none of which accepted him. Instead, our local authority, in its wisdom, allocated him a placement at what is arguably one of the worst schools in our borough, a school that in my view, is a monument to underachievement, and where bullies notoriously rule the hallways. We knew that sending him there would be the equivalent of writing him off, and so we were forced to dig deep into our savings and send him to a private school. He's a very sensitive child and not at all streetwise, and is one of those kids who would just have been a bully magnet. I shudder to think what would have happened if we had not been able to make that choice.

# Property ownership

In order to show how important **ownership** is in a capitalist society, let's have a look at a concept that we can all relate to – property ownership.

We know that different 'levels' of ownership afford us different levels of rights and power, and indeed, opportunity.

Most people's greatest aspiration where property is concerned, is to own their own property outright (and well done to those of you who do).

Second best is to own a freehold with a mortgage on it. This is more an 'illusion' of ownership.

Did you know that, in theory at least, a mortgaged property can be repossessed from the moment the mortgage is created? In fact, in a legal case called *Four Maids Ltd v Dudley Marshall Properties Ltd* ([1957] Ch. 317), Judge Harman J held that *'The mortgagee may go into possession before the ink is dry on the mortgage, unless there is something in the contract, express or implied, whereby he has contracted himself out of that right'*.[5]

In reality, thankfully this hardly ever happens, but if you miss a few mortgage payments then you will discover who **really** owns the property. But it's a strong illusion and it works well.

The third level is to own a leasehold property. The rules of possession still apply but, as those of us who own leaseholds have discovered, though this level of ownership is better than none, potentially we can become enslaved to the freeholder. That's because, although we may own the structure, we do not own the land on which it stands, which is why service charges can be hiked almost arbitrarily and there's not much we can do about it as long as they are considered 'reasonable' in law.

The value of property ownership should not be underestimated, though. Because you **own** the property, you can pretty much do what you want with it without getting consent from a landlord. More importantly, you can do things to it that make it go up in value – something as simple as painting it can increase the value – which translates into **profit** (and you thought you weren't a capitalist!).

If you keep up your payments, it can also greatly increase your credit rating.

An important note to make here is that, because in a capitalist society **ownership is everything, rent money is dead money**. (Yes, I know there are exceptions to that rule, but that is the general rule of thumb.)

Rent money affords you very few rights and those that you have are not transferable; for instance, you cannot leave a rented flat to your children, which is why the fact that a whole generation of young people are finding it practically impossible to get on the property ladder should be a source of panic to them, because that means one of the best ways in which they can have a financial stake in society, or a slice of the financial cake, is increasingly no longer open to them.

Just think about this. If a tenant & a homeowner who has kept up the mortgage payments in a timely fashion for a number of years (thus demonstrating good financial management), both apply to their local bank for a loan to set up a business, who do you think they are going to give it to? It's a no-brainer. **Ownership is everything!**

But enough about property. Now that we have a slightly better understanding of the importance of ownership, let's take the concept into the world of work.

# Ownership and the workplace

Just as the ideal is to own your own property outright, in the world of work what would be ideal is for you to own your own profitable business (or businesses), and it doesn't have to be a large business to make you a lot of money.

In the United States, research shows that less than 20% of the working population own their own business, but those who do make up more than two-thirds of the millionaires. Again, **business ownership** translates into **profit** for the owners.

Where you cannot be an **owner** of a business, you should be a shareholder in a business.

Shareholders are **owners of the company**, or **own** parts of a limited company, and their rights vary from country to country.

Under UK law, shareholder rights are very strong and include the rights to: vote for directors; vote on or initiate changes to the company articles or laws that govern the company; vote on or initiate proposed fundamental changes, such as mergers or dissolutions; vote on proposed dividends; participate in shareholder meetings; and pre-emptively purchase newly issued shares.

The degree of **ownership** of any shareholder is determined by how many shares of the company they own.

As I said earlier, it is imperative that you have various income streams, and being a shareholder is one of those streams.

In the absence of the above, you should be looking to be a **stakeholder**.

On the internet you will find numerous definitions of a 'stakeholder', but in the context of which I'm speaking, a stakeholder is someone who has particular skills, knowledge, expertise, or contacts that are imperative to the continued success of a company. You know the kind of people you read about in the papers who are paid a £1m 'golden hello'. Those people have established themselves so well within a particular industry that they are able to negotiate such a package – and I use the word package on purpose, because often the salary (which is usually eye-watering in itself), is actually the least important item within the package. There will be the share options, the holiday home, the bonus, generous annual leave and the protected pension; even the salary will be linked to the consumer prices index or the retail prices index (I'll explain what those are later). Their knowledge, skills and contacts are such that they are able to exercise negotiation and decision-making power over their own terms and conditions in the workplace, something the majority of the working class are unable to do. Such is that power that, even when their performance doesn't live up to the hype (which is not unusual), just to get rid of them you have to pay them, and they usually leave with all their benefits intact!

> To be wholly dependent on a salary in a capitalist society not only makes you perpetually vulnerable, it's tantamount to economic suicide.

Now, I have a no-brainer question for you, but it's important that you answer it.

**If you are not a business owner, a shareholder, or a stakeholder in a capitalist society, where ownership is everything, do you think that being a mere worker (dependent on a salary) puts you in a position of weakness or a position of strength?**

As I said, it's a no-brainer. In the workplace, **if you are not an owner, you are an outsider,** no matter how far up the corporate food chain you go. To be wholly dependent on a salary in a capitalist society not only makes you perpetually vulnerable, it's tantamount to economic suicide.

'But a job provides security', I hear you cry. No! Security is a concept that is often thought to be synonymous with freedom. Actually, **security is the price an employee pays for freedom**, financial and otherwise. Confusing those two concepts can keep you in financial bondage for the rest of your life.

The bottom line is this:

**As a 21st-century employee, you can no longer afford to single-mindedly serve your employer without taking active steps to establish different income streams and create, grow and protect your own wealth, thus safeguarding your own financial future.**

Hopefully this book, and others like it, will arm you with the tools you need to do just that.

---

To purchase my six-part live seminar series 'How to create, grow and protect your wealth' for the special price of £45, visit www.bebeclement.com/shop and enter code **ET1**

---

# CHAPTER 2

*And just when you thought it couldn't get any worse...*

In a capitalist society there are three main groups of people: producers, distributors and consumers.

1. **Producers** are those who make or create something that adds sufficient value to somebody's life, such that they are willing to pay you for it. Please note: **producers are not just people who have something to sell**. Rather, they have a product that answers a question in somebody's life or meets a need.

   **I am a producer.** What do I produce? I produce knowledge. I put my knowledge on a CD, DVD, digital download, in a book, or convey it during a seminar; and people pay for it because it adds value to their life.

2. **Distributors** bring demand and supply together. For example, one of our businesses is a law firm that caters specifically for the needs of small businesses. One of our clients owns a large African cash and carry. He imports African foodstuffs such as rice, black-eyed beans and *gari* for UK-based Africans. The demand is created by Africans in the UK and the supply is the African foodstuffs.

   **I am a distributor.** When I hold a seminar or workshop, I bring together the supply (those who attend my seminars) and the demand (whatever topic I am speaking on at that event).

3. **Consumers** inevitably, in some context or another, include all of us, but I want to give consumers a slightly narrower definition here. Please read the following carefully and maybe you'll recognise yourself in my description.

Consumers have a lot of debt, and lots of credit cards, store cards etc. They owe money and have poor money-management skills. They wear the latest designer clothes but **own** very little. They drive a flashy car (but it's bought on credit and they often park it in front of a council flat that they do not own). They have only one source of income – usually their salary. Financially, they would not last six months without a job. They usually have little or no savings and, if they were to drop dead today, their children and loved ones would discover that they had made very little provision for them. In other words, they merely look the part.

**It's a pity that what the working class often mistakes for 'success' is, on closer inspection, nothing other than a high-consumption lifestyle.**

The secret to thriving (not just surviving) in a capitalist society is that you must fit into at least two of the categories in the list above. The tragedy for most of the working class is that they are only found in the third category, as consumers. Consumers find it difficult to avoid the destructive pull of instant gratification and they usually don't know the difference between **money** and **wealth**.

Money may mean a Rolex on the wrist and a flashy car, but wealth is being able to send your children to the best schools, thereby securing their future; having healthy savings, and sufficient income to comfortably pay the mortgage and contribute to a pension plan, with enough left over to donate to charity and be a financial blessing to friends, family and the wider society. Money is a flash in the pan; wealth is forever.

Now, before you get mad at me, address the following questions to yourself and answer honestly:

What am I **producing**?

What am I **distributing**?

Am I just a **consumer**?

If your answer to either 1 or 2 was **nothing**, please hear me when I say you are well on your way to becoming a casualty of a capitalist society, and alarm bells should be ringing in your ears by now.

Let me ask you another question. If you were to lose your job today, how long could you last without having to borrow money or apply for social security benefits? A year? Six months? Three months? Many of us couldn't even last that long, and all you need is one major financial mishap during that period (like the boiler packs up) and that redundancy payment goes up in smoke. It's a bleak picture, isn't it? But wait, there's more!

# CHAPTER 3

# *Consumer price index*

I know you will have heard of the consumer price index or CPI (it's on the news all the time), but do you know what it is and do you understand its importance in your life as a 21st-century worker in a capitalist society? Don't worry, I didn't either, and I'm grateful to my good friend, Dr Remi Banjoko, for enlightening me during one of our joint one-day seminars on wealth creation.

Every month, the government does an analysis of the **basic** cost of living for the average Joe living in the UK. This is how it works.

The government takes a notional 'basket of goods' that represents typical UK household spending and analyses the cost. For example, it will reckon that the average Joe wakes up in a bed that costs about £300. He will be wearing a pair of pyjamas that would have cost him about £20. He then gets up and puts on his slippers (£10) and totters to the kitchen of his one-bedroom flat that costs £800 monthly rent. He then puts on the kettle (that cost him £20) and makes a cup of black coffee (£3 a packet). I have no idea of the actual cost of these things, but you get the picture.

In this way, it then works out the average price of **basic** daily living every month and whether prices have risen or fallen. Taking the figures over a whole year, the basic cost of living can then be compared from one year to the next. As at the time of writing, the CPI for the UK is 0.6%. This means that **you have to pay 0.6% more this year for the same basket of goods than you would have paid this time, last year**. Get it?

Now, in order for you to thrive in whatever financial endeavour you are involved in (be it wages, investments, business or something else), you must be earning at least 2% above the CPI at any given time.

So here's another question for you. By what percentage was your salary last increased?

The last time I asked this question during one of my wealth creation seminars, the response in the main was 'None. My salary has been frozen'. (Public servants in particular, you have my sympathies!) If that is the case for you, the CPI is 0.6% and your salary increase was 0%. Can you see that you are already starting from behind and you haven't even bought anything yet?

If your salary increase (or any financial endeavours you are involved in) is not at least 2.6%, **you are wasting your time!** You are like someone running up an escalator that is going down. Do you know how much time and effort is required to do that, to just keep going? There is a huge difference between motion and movement. A rocking horse is constantly in motion, but it's not moving anywhere, and sadly, many of us get to the end of our working lives and discover that we have been in economic motion for most of it but have made no movement.

# CHAPTER 4

## *Scared, but prepared*

A constant feedback from delegates who attend my wealth creation seminars is that the information I present scares them stiff. I make no apology for that. In fact, it tells me I am doing my job properly.

Many of us are lackadaisical about our financial situation because we don't have a proper grasp of the dire facts. Hopefully you now have a clearer picture of the sinking sand on which you stand. But really, it's not my aim to **scare you**; but it **is** my aim to **prepare you**. So, now that you know the facts, **what are you going to do about it**?

As I said earlier, the solution, as I see it, is to **own**. **Own** land, **own** property, **own** shares, **own** a small business, **own** investments, develop different income streams; the more the better. (I read recently that the average millionaire has at least seven sources of income at any given time.) Anything legal that you can do that brings in money, do it! But **doing nothing is just not an option**.

There are others better equipped than I to show you how to do all the aforementioned, but I want to concentrate on how to use a small business as a source of ownership or an income stream.

# CHAPTER 5

# *The small business as an income stream*

I quoted an interesting statistic earlier. Apparently, less than 20% of the US workforce own their own business, but those who do make up over two-thirds of the millionaires in that country. Amazing huh? More importantly, it proves that there is a direct correlation between wealth creation and entrepreneurship. Research shows that you don't have to own a large business to become wealthy. A number of small business owners are millionaires. (I'm hoping to join that number soon.)

## Getting started

There are a number of definitions for the word *entrepreneur*, and I'm sure you've heard many of them, but my favourite is this:

**An entrepreneur is someone who turns *passion* into *profit*.**

I'll come back to that, but first of all, what is your gift? Your gift or talent will very often be the gateway to your financial freedom. Your gift is something that comes naturally to you. Something that you make look easy, whereas other people would struggle to do it, and when you do it, it gives you a sense of fulfilment and joy.

For example, they tell me that the fear of public speaking is one of the greatest fears known to man (often featuring higher than a fear of death), but it's something I have no difficulty in doing, (once I get past the butterflies in my stomach), and my sold-out seminars and other programmes would suggest that I do it well.

But, your gift is not enough. Your gift should be undergirded by your passion. So what are you passionate about? If your answer to that question is 'I don't really know', here's a good test.

Most people are unable to pursue their dreams because they are weighed down by the demands of life. The mortgage, the kids, financial obligations, the expectations of loved ones and friends, the fear of failure, the list goes on. All contribute to keeping us stuck in mediocrity.

But imagine that you could lay all that down, and that you were able to live your life over, knowing what you know now. What would you do? Even if no one saw you doing it, nobody congratulated or rewarded you and nobody paid you, would you still do it? **That is your passion!** Think of someone like Beyoncé. I bet if that beautiful woman was dropped on a desert island, she would just line up the coconuts in rows like an audience and sing and dance to her heart's content, because that's her lifelong passion. She was born to do it!

What you need to do is match your gift to your passion and you are bound to come up with a business idea. Luckily for you, you are multi-gifted, so you will probably discover that you will emerge with more than one idea. Write them all down and see what you come up with.

Here's what mine looked like a few years ago.

| Gifts/talents | Knowledge/experience | Passion |
|---|---|---|
| Good public speaking skills | Employment law | Seeing people 'put their signature on life', irrespective of the hand life has dealt them, and arming them with the tools with which to do so |
| | HR | |
| Natural leader | Christianity | |
| Excellent event organising skills | Leadership | |
| | Business start-ups | |
| | Community organising | |
| | Life skills (over-coming tragedy) | |

Out of the above exercise came two businesses: a legal consultancy specialising in employment law, and an international speaking and training company – and now this book!

## Passion is the key!

I cannot emphasise enough the importance of making sure that any business you start off with is one that you are passionate about. When you grow and become more established and wealthy you can diversify into other businesses and income streams, but not at that initial stage.

Why is passion so important? Because I've discovered that people *buy* passion. In other words, **passion sells**!

Generally, we live in a world of 'same old, same old', but people with passion buck that trend. They have a fire in their belly which is reflected in their eyes. They are infectious and impossible to ignore. Passion is contagious! In other words, people are **influenced** by passion. Influence is the ability to move someone in a particular direction, in this case, to purchase your product, whatever that may be. That's why it is actually easier to sell a crappy product with passion than it is to sell a great product in a lacklustre manner.

Another reason passion is so important is that it is your passion that sees you through the dark and lonely nights in business. The days when everything that can possibly go wrong does and you feel like giving up (and believe me there are many days like that in business). The light of passion can be dimmed, but it's very difficult to put out. Somehow, the entrepreneur is able to fan a flicker into flame and go on.

## Stop waiting for pay day

I must give a word of warning here.

I have met many people who, given the chance, would be very successful (not to talk of rich), if they would only follow their passion, but one of the things that deters them is that they are doing what I call 'waiting for pay day'. What I mean by that is this:

It is not unusual for you to find that, when you discover your passion, it is a million miles away from the job you are currently doing, or the activities you are involved in right now, or, totally different from what you studied at university. Having spent all that time pursuing your career and landing your current job, you are scared that if you go off and do something else with your life, (even though you have an inner witness that this is what you were born to do) then somehow you will miss the pay-off for all your hard work.

For example, supposing your parents and teachers recognised that you had a head for figures at a young age and encouraged you to go into accountancy. You studied for three years at university, got a job as an Accounts Assistant, got promoted after three years, during which time you were doing the professional exams, and finally qualified as a chartered accountant. You then got a job in a top accountancy firm and have been steadily climbing up the corporate ladder ever since. They like you, and there have been whispers that, if you play your cards right, you might be the next chief accountant of the firm.

But deep down you have always had a passion for baking cakes. Out of sheer love you have baked cakes for friends in the past and they have always loved them. You've listened to their guests ooh and aah at parties over your cakes and watched in amazement as people asked for the phone number of the person who made the cake so they could order their child's next birthday cake from them. But even though deep down, you know that you actually hate working in an office, can't stand your boss and would love nothing more than to ice cakes all day, how could you walk away from all you have invested in becoming the accountant you are? Besides, it would break your mother's heart. So you decide to stay because you are waiting for your investment to pay off, not just for financial reasons, but because of the years and effort you have put into it.

The fear of losing that investment keeps many people in a job or career they hate.

My dear friend, if that investment was going to pay off, it would have done so by now. There are some things in life that you just have to draw a line under, write off as a bad debt and take the risk of pursuing what is really in your heart. You have a limited number of years on this earth. Too short to waste precious time being and doing something other than what you were born to be and do.

Once you've discovered your passion, find a way to package it into a commodity. You may need some help with this from someone like me, who can sit down with you and help you get your thoughts in order.

As I said above, my favourite definition of an entrepreneur is someone who can **turn passion into profit**.

Usually when we hear the word profit we think of money, but it's more than that. It also means being able to add value to your life and the lives of others.

When you do something you are passionate about, it has an amazing, positive effect on your health, sense of well-being and sense of achievement, not to mention your creativity levels. As the saying goes, practice makes perfect, and the more time you spend on a daily basis working on and crafting a business you are passionate about, the better it becomes – and your customers will be better off for it.

> You have a limited number of years on this earth. Too short to waste precious time being and doing something other than what you were born to be and do.

# CHAPTER 6

# *Who wants to be an entrepreneur (and why)?*

Let's be honest, not everyone is cut out to be an entrepreneur, so it's important to examine the reasons **why** you want to go into business. Research shows that the reasons behind why someone goes into business go a long way in determining whether they will succeed.

Various studies (such as Bosma and Harding, 2007[1]) have found that people who go into business generally fall into two groups – the 'push' group and the 'pull' group.

**The pull group** are people who go into business for the following reasons:

- they want to be their own boss
- they want to be independent and make money
- they spot a market opportunity
- they want to be in control of their own and their family's future.

**The push group** are people who go into business for the following reasons:

- they have been made redundant or are unemployed
- they want to overcome social exclusion
- they have family commitments requiring flexibility.

Research suggests that those in the pull group tend to do better in business. They are more likely to invest substantial amounts of capital into their business, be better equipped with the skills and belief system needed to succeed in business (such as tenacity), and more likely to create further job opportunities as the business grows.

In contrast, those in the push group tend to invest less, have lower expectations of success, are unlikely to create further employment, and show less innovation in the way they do business.

The reasons for this are not that far-reaching: generally people who do things out of intrinsic desire (the pull group) rather than external pressure or lack of choice, such as the threat of unemployment (the push group), tend to do better.

However, there is a subgroup that research suggests tends to do worst of all. Can you guess who might be in that group? It's those who start a business for reasons relating to family commitments that require flexibility. Maybe the following example will reveal why that is.

Let's say I have two young children under the age of 5, Olu and Ade. My high-powered legal job means that I keep missing their school plays and I hardly ever get home from work before bedtime. After a couple of years my husband and I decide this is not sustainable and, more importantly, not fair to the kids, so we decide that I should resign and go into business for myself.

I've always wanted to own a newsagent and convenience store. My local one is always packed and it seems like a good business to get into. So, I buy into a franchise and open my shop. I know I won't be able to afford a shop assistant initially, so I'll be running it myself.

When I resigned from my job, we agreed that we no longer needed an au pair, but as my husband still has to leave for work early, it's now left to me to get the kids ready and drop them off at school every morning. As you know, newsagents are heavily dependent on early morning foot trade – people buying newspapers, travel cards, snacks and drinks for work etc. – but because I have to drop off the kids, I miss a lot of that trade.

Then one day little Ade comes home from school with a note from his class teacher. Apparently, while he was changing for PE, his teacher noticed a couple of nasty spots on his chest. *Could I please take him to the doctor to ensure he doesn't have chicken pox?*

This I do, and the doctor confirms that little Ade does indeed have chicken pox and he is not allowed to go to school for at least five days. The doctor also warns me that I should keep him away from the general public, and particularly from pregnant women. That means that I can't take little Ade to the shop after school as I usually do when I pick them both up in the afternoon. Instead, I will have to close the shop until he recovers.

See what I mean? In the example above, the reason for which I went into business is the very reason for which the business failed – family commitments. Now, that doesn't mean everyone who starts a business for that reason will automatically fail, but it is very important that people who have family commitments and wish to go into business ensure they have made sufficient provision for their family, (in this case adequate childcare), so it does not get in the way.

From personal experience, a **lot** of discipline is required to make a small business work.

My husband and I run a group of small businesses, one of which I run from home, so we get the kids ready in the morning and then he leaves to oversee our law firm, where he is the principal. I do a bit of housework, shower, then I start work around 9am and usually work through till the kids get back at about 4pm. Then it's dinner, homework and play, often interspersed with more work throughout the evening.

The key is to resist the temptation to switch on the TV or pick up the phone to speak to friends. If you absolutely need to, then keep it short. It's hard, but it can be done!

# CHAPTER 7

*Businesses
don't plan to fail,
they just fail to plan!*

I'm sure you've heard that said before – and it's true.

Think about this. You wouldn't apply for a job without checking basic details such as the salary, the hours required, the geographical location and, equally importantly, whether you have what it takes to fulfil the requirements of the job; so it amazes me the number of people who go into business just because they have what they think is a good business idea, without taking the time to probe a little deeper.

## Market research

Market research may be tedious and time-consuming but, let me tell you, even if it takes you two years to carry out, you are better off taking the time to do it – even if you discover at the end that your business idea is not viable – than plunging headlong into a business only to reach the same conclusion after expending considerable time, and usually money.

Your market research gives you vital information about your proposed business. *Is there actually a market for this product? If so, who wants it? How much are they willing to pay for it? Do I need an office or can I run it from my kitchen table? What kind of professional assistance do I need?* And so on.

Whatever market research you do should be customer-focussed. After all, it is the customer who will determine whether you have a business, so here are the kinds of questions you should be asking:

## Who are my customers?

Let's start off with some myth busting – **the whole world is my customer.**

No, it's not!

Even if you are selling something as universal as water, that rule still applies. Supposing you are selling bottled water: some people like fizzy water, some still, others flavoured, others coloured, and some tap water. No matter your product, you have a demographic. You must find out what it is and aim your product at that group.

## Where are they?

It is unlikely that your customers are going to come looking for you. Even internet-based companies still have to put something in front of their target audience to attract buyers to their sales sites. So, if customers won't come to you, you must go to them. But you can only do that if you know where they are.

Identifying or determining your target audience or customer will go a long way in helping you find out where your customers are.

For instance, if I were the owner of a cash and carry selling African food on a large scale to Africans in London and was given a shop rent-free in the middle of Chelsea, there is no point in me going to set up shop there because that's not where my customers are. They are in Peckham, Woolwich, Thamesmead, Brixton – anywhere that large numbers of Africans reside – so, that's where my business should be.

With the advancement of the internet and online shopping, of course, answering the question 'Where are my customers?' is no longer just a question of geographical location. Perhaps more important is determining where your customers are and where they are visiting online. Once you have discovered that, you need to set up a strong presence there.

As you know, there are many social media platforms that you can use to promote your business, but I'm just briefly going to talk about the three I think are most important to small businesses in particular, namely Facebook, Twitter and LinkedIn.

Say, for example, your potential customers are young people, then Facebook (and increasingly Instagram) would probably be your best bet for finding customers, because that currently seems to be the most popular platform with them. In a recent survey of 7,000 young people, 61% said they visited Facebook daily.

Likewise, one of the businesses my husband and I run is a legal magazine called *Law Digest*. As our magazine is targeted towards professionals, we have a strong presence on LinkedIn because that's where our customers for this particular product are.

In order to build awareness of our brand, stay in the consciousness of our customers and, of course, drive sales for our magazine, we initiate and contribute to legal debates and topics that may be of interest to them, thereby setting ourselves up as the experts or the 'go-to' people in our field, and that's what you need to do.

> To view *Law Digest* online or make enquiries about our conferences and award nights, visit www.nglawdigest.com.

When I first started the employment law consultancy, I established that my target audience was small businesses and employees. I made a list of all the small businesses in my neighbourhood and decided to pay them a visit to introduce my services.

I must admit I found this very daunting. I was very nervous, but I felt I could explain my services better face to face. I believe that physically visiting customer sites gives you a better feel for their business. Also, they are on home turf, so they are comfortable and usually more willing to talk, and you can sometimes discover other needs or problems they have that your services can assist with.

I'll never forget the very first business I visited, which was a care agency. I walked in and asked to see the MD, explaining that I had just started a local employment law consultancy and just wanted to introduce myself and my services.

As fate would have it, the MD was on site. *Yes, she had a few minutes to spare if I could make it brief.* I introduced myself and the services I had to offer that I thought would benefit a company like hers.

As I was speaking she began to giggle. As I went on it became full-blown, desk-thumping laughter. It was very off-putting and I was very embarrassed. In the end I couldn't take it any longer and asked her why she found my spiel so hilarious.

When she had calmed down she explained that I could not have timed it better. There were some problems brewing in her company and that very morning, she had said to her managers that it had now come to the stage where she needed legal advice on some specific matters. She would also need ongoing advice because she now had so many staff that she needed the services of an HR company to assist with employee-related issues. She further explained that she needed help with nearly everything I had highlighted in my introduction. She wanted to sign me up there and then! I said I'd get back to her because, to be honest, I hadn't expected that response, so I hadn't brought any paperwork, but we talked a little longer and we formally outlined her requirements. I went away and worked on drawing up a retainer package, returned the next day, and she signed the documentation.

That woman was one of my best customers over the next few years. Not only did she own a care agency, she also owned care homes, a security firm and some other businesses, so she kept me pretty busy over the next few years.

# What do my customers do?

You should find out what your potential customers spend their time doing. Where do they hang out? What do they read?

A really good example comes to mind of a friend who started a business magazine for high-net-worth businesspeople in Nigeria.

His market research revealed to him that his target customers were often members of a particular country club, which not only was he not a member of, but he had never been to. The chances of him becoming a member were almost non-existent as he did not fulfil the membership criteria of having several millions in the bank. He discovered, however, that he could attend as a visitor if he was invited by a club member. He got himself invited and devised a plan.

He observed that many of the waiters had worked there for several years and knew most of the members by name. So, he made friends with a couple of them, asked for their help in promoting his magazine and offered to pay for their assistance.

He selected a list of members that he wanted to get his magazine in front of.

The plan was, when serving these members, the waiter would casually ask whether they had seen this magazine and hand them a free copy. Once they observed that the member had read it, they would ask if they had enjoyed it and ask their opinion about it. This information was then filtered back to my friend, who began to fashion the magazine based on the comments he received.

Then when a particular member seemed particularly impressed by the magazine, the waiter would find out when they would next be at the club and inform my friend who would casually turn up at the club at the opportune time. The waiter would then say to the member, something like, 'By the way, the editor of that magazine you liked last week is sitting at the bar. Would you like to meet him?' And that's how my friend gained access to his target audience. Today, people are clamouring to be featured in his magazines, and he now owns a number of industry-themed publications.

## What do they need?

Notice the question is **what do they need**? It's not asking what do you **think** they need.

A few years ago, watching property makeover programmes was one of my greatest pastimes.

There was a particular programme, *Property Ladder* that followed budding property developers who would purchase run-down homes and do them up to sell for a profit.

One of the classic mistakes many of the property developers would make was that somewhere along the way they would forget why they were doing what they were doing and, more importantly, who they were doing it for.

For instance, when shopping for a new kitchen to install in the property, they would come across a really expensive bespoke kitchen and decide they wanted it. Sarah Beeny, the presenter, would try to steer them back to the fact that the kitchen was way too expensive and might not be what their prospective buyers **needed** in their new property. More importantly, she pointed out that, even though it cost a bomb (say 20k), it would not add that much more value, (if any), to the property, and so, was an unnecessary expense that would simply reduce their profit, and that a £3,000 kitchen from the likes of B&Q would achieve the aim of updating the house at a much lower cost.

The reaction of some of the developers was very interesting and revealed a classic mistake made by new entrepreneurs. They would say things such as 'I like this kitchen. It's the kind of kitchen I would like in a house that I was going to live in.' And that's the whole point. They were not doing up a house for **them** to live in; they should have been doing it up in the way that would appeal to their prospective buyers. In other words, they should have been asking 'What do my potential buyers **need**?'

Often in the programme, once the property was ready for sale, they would secretly film prospective buyers as they walked round and viewed the property, deciding whether to buy it.

It was amazing the number who would say something like, 'I like the house, but the kitchen looks out of place.' In effect, the thing that the seller thought would be the gold star in the property would be the very thing that would stop them from making a sale. Why? Because they did not understand their customers' **needs**.

The worst thing an entrepreneur can do is to **assume** to know what the customer wants. You need to find out for sure!

To further the point, let me give a personal example. I am from Nigeria and, once in a while, my family and I go out to enjoy food at a Nigerian restaurant.

In the area where I live, there are three Nigerian restaurants within about a three-mile radius, but we bypass all of them and go to a restaurant that takes us about 30 minutes to drive to. The food at our chosen restaurant is not any tastier than those in our neighbourhood and, per head, it is on average about £5 more expensive.

But we choose to go there because:

1.   I like the ambiance. The decor is nice and it's very clean.

2.  The service is fast. I have an autistic son, and anyone familiar with autism knows that waiting is not a strong point, so it's important to us that the food arrives in a timely fashion.

3.  The restaurant has a family feel. They play a lot of Nigerian music, which my children love, and it's not unusual for my children to get up and dance. This does not faze the staff at all, so no snooty waiter will come over and ask me to control my children!

If you were going to open a Nigerian restaurant and you **assumed** that costing the average plate at £8,instead of £10 like your competitors, would win my business, you would be sorely mistaken because price or cost is actually the least important factor in the equation. Bottom line: don't assume to know what your customers need. **Find out**.

One of the best ways to find out what people want is to ask questions, particularly the question, **why**? You see, asking what people want is pretty basic. If someone wants to buy some soap from you, clearly that's what they want. But the question, **why**? usually reveals the underlying reasoning behind their decision to purchase that product, which is much more important. Then you can find out the **value** of that product to the customer, and indeed other problems that they may have. For instance, if you ask 'Why do you want to buy this soap?', you might discover that they have an aversion to perfumed soaps, whereas this one has no smell, or they may have a problem with acne that this soap addresses. You may then be able to sell them some cleanser that they can apply before using the soap and a cream that they can apply following the cleansing. At the end of the day, you could end up selling the customer three products when ordinarily they would have purchased only one, simply because you asked the question **why**?

## Tell me what you want, what you really, really want!

In finding out what people need, you must also be aware that sometimes they don't know what they need.

Henry Ford said if he had asked people what they wanted, they would have said faster horses, when really, they needed a completely different mode of transport – cars. Now this does not negate the need to ask questions. I'm just showing you the other side of the coin.

The majority of people making money in the current system do so because they understand that sometimes it is the job of an entrepreneur to **educate** customers about what they need. One of the most effective ways to do this is to present them with a problem or challenge that they are unaware of. I highlight a 'disconnect' between where the customer is and where they need to be, and show them that my products and services are the 'bridge'. That's pretty much what I am doing with this book. Most people are unaware **why**, despite their best efforts, they can't seem to make ends meet. My job is to show you that working your butt off for a promotion and salary increase, or even looking for a different job, is not the solution. In order to be financially free, **you must own** and have different income streams.

## How can I communicate to my customers that I can meet their needs?

First of all you have to speak their language. I don't mean that literally; I mean you need to know **what** to say to your customers and **how** to say it in a way that will resonate and influence them to buy your product.

One of my areas of expertise and passion is leadership. I believe that the success of any business, organisation or indeed, nation, rises and falls on the quality of leadership. I therefore offer leadership training to companies, church leaders and young people.

There is a particular leadership training package I offer where the material is basically the same for these three groups of people, but I simply tweak it to suit. Even if I were going to offer the exact same content to these three groups, the keywords that I would use on the flyers or marketing material would be different.

---

To book leadership training or get information on other training packages that I offer, visit www.bebeclement.com/training.

---

If I were marketing my leadership training to young people, I might say something like this on the flyer or marketing material:

### Be there. It's gonna be dope!

Every young person knows that 'dope' means **great** or really good. That's their language.

Clearly, if I were creating a flyer for church leaders, I wouldn't have 'dope' anywhere on it. They might think I'm selling drugs!

In addition, if I were going to advertise the leadership programme to young people I would do so on Facebook or Instagram. Why? Because they are the Facebook generation: that's their social media platform and the 'language' used on these platforms requires less formality or is less formal. Even when they are professionals, young people hardly ever visit sites like LinkedIn.

However, if I wanted to market the leadership package to senior managers or company directors, I would probably do so on LinkedIn.

Knowing how to communicate with your customers goes even further.

A few years ago I was asked to organise a women's business breakfast meeting in my church. As it was a business event, people were able to hire stands to showcase their products.

The women attending were mainly professionals, had healthy disposable incomes and were used to high standards.

A woman approached me who sold cosmetics. She asked if she could do a makeover during the meeting to showcase her cosmetics so she could sell them afterwards. I agreed.

During the presentation it became clear that she was not prepared. Rather than bringing a model along, she asked for a volunteer from the delegates. It took ages for her to persuade someone to be the guinea pig.

Part of her presentation included wiping off an overnight cream from the volunteer's face to apply some day cream. She had forgotten the container for dipping the cotton cleaning pad in and improvised using water in a plastic cup. I watched the looks of horror on the women's faces and knew she would not sell any products there that day; not because the product itself was bad (in fact, it was a very good product range which I use myself), but because the 'language' of her potential customers was one of high expectations and professionalism, and the language she had spoken to them was shoddiness, unpreparedness and 'make do'. As a result, she had failed to make a connection with her potential customers and was unable to influence them into buying her product.

A final word on customers...

# The 80/20 rule

The 80/20 rule states that 80% of your income will come from 20% of your customers.

Conversely, you will find that the majority of your customers from whom you make very little money are the ones who actually take up most of your time, and as time is your greatest resource, this is to be avoided at all costs. Don't make the mistake of thinking that if you spend more time speaking to a customer whenever they call and want to talk about their dog, then they will buy more products. It's not true. Commit to providing excellent service as a rule, but understand that, no matter what you do, some people just like to moan and want you to be at their beck and call; and strangely, it doesn't increase their patronage.

It is therefore imperative that, very early on, you identify the 20% money-makers and look for innovative ways to expand the services you provide for them.

As you know, one of our companies is a legal consultancy, providing employment law and HR services to SMEs. When one of my clients was having issues with two members of staff who were not getting along, a situation that had a negative impact on wider staff morale, we expanded our services to include mediation, which they happily bought into. We now offer this service to other clients.

Another reason why this is important is because research shows that it costs between 5 and 10 times more in terms of money, effort and time to recruit new customers than to get repeat business from an existing customer (eMarketer, 2002[1]). So, offer such great service to your customers as to make yourself irreplaceable, and keep looking for ways to add value to what you offer your existing paying customers.

## Who are your competitors?

You need to find out what your competitors are offering and see how you can do it better. Don't be afraid to 'steal' a competitor's way of doing things if it works (but obviously not their actual product or intellectual property!). Steve Jobs famously said this: 'We have always been shameless about stealing great ideas.'[2]

One of the myths among SMEs is that, in order to grow your client base, you must undercut your competitors in the area of price. This is simply not true. You need to find out how you can offer what your competitors are offering, but find a way to do it better.

> Your product should be solving problems or meeting needs. Once it is doing that – in other words, when it is **adding value** – people will buy it, even if it does cost that bit more.

Besides, as the restaurant example above shows, unless you know exactly what part of your offer the customer needs and is willing to pay for, it's difficult to know what price to put on it.

# Finance

Another thing market research will help you identify is how much money you need to get the business off the ground. These are some of the things that you will need money for.

## Working capital

This is what you need to keep the business ticking over on a day-to-day basis. It includes funds for staff (if you have any), stationery, marketing, rent, transport, professional services, bills, hospitality.

A word about professional services: you need them. Get over it! They may be expensive, but they are so for a reason. Don't scrimp on them. Get the best you can afford. Proven recommendations are the way to go.

## Capital investment

This is more of your heavy-duty, long-term financial investment; in IT and telephone systems, heavy machinery, manufacturing plants and the like.

Since we are on the topic of finance, once you have established how much you will need to get the business off the ground and keep it running, you then need to look at ways to raise that sum.

# How to raise finance

## Personal assets

This is where the importance of **ownership** really kicks in. Most businesses need some level of capital in order to get off the ground. To raise capital (particularly from a bank) you need collateral. In other words, you must **own** something that the bank can recover value from if the investment goes belly up.

In the example I gave in chapter one, it is a no-brainer that, if two prospective business owners approach a bank for a loan, and one owns nothing and lives in rented accommodation, while the other has diligently paid their mortgage on a property they own, the bank is more likely to give the loan to the property owner.

Also, if you **own** different income streams, not only can you borrow against them, you can liquidate them to invest in the business. For instance, if you are a shareholder you can sell some shares or a piece of land to raise funds for your new business.

## Angel investors

There is a TV programme in the UK called *Dragon's Den* (which originated in Japan and has other versions in different countries).

The contestants are usually product designers or service operators who have what they consider to be a viable and potentially profitable business idea, but lack funding and direction. They pitch their idea to five rich entrepreneurial businesspeople or 'angel investors'. The contestants ask for a specific amount of money in exchange for a percentage of the business profits.

For most budding entrepreneurs the input of angel investors makes the difference between getting a business off the ground and watching their dream of starting such a business die.

This route also has the advantage of enabling quick investment decisions. There is no need for collateral or personal assets and, unlike a normal bank loan, there are no repayments or interest payable.

A word of caution: some angel investors have been proven to be devils in disguise because they don't just bring the finance to the table; they also bring expertise and, more importantly, their industry contacts. It is not unheard of for them to grow the business to a particular size and then elbow the original owner out of the door. Some business owners have been discredited within the industry by their so-called angels, thus finding it difficult to ever operate a business in that industry again. So, beware!

## Family and friends

Most people underestimate family and friends as a potential fundraising stream. You would be amazed at the number of people who are sitting on a load of capital but don't know what to do with it, so don't be afraid to ask!

However, another word of caution: money is a great source of relationship breakdown. Even though you may be getting the money from your great aunt Edna and it's all done very informally, always remember that **it is a business relationship**. Make sure there is a legal agreement in place. This will ensure that any confusion or misconceptions are dealt with and don't lead to family conflicts or fallouts.

## Credit cards

I am actually loath to recommend this as a source of raising capital because most people do not have the discipline required for repaying money borrowed on credit, and because the interest rate is usually quite high (18% on average).

Having said that, some credit card companies offer 0% repayment periods. In other words, an interest-free loan, **provided** you clear your balance before the 0% offer ends. For some business owners it is a lifesaver, but make sure you have the discipline to make it work for you.

## Banks

You will have noticed that I have not yet recommended banks as a means of raising capital. This is deliberate. It's not impossible to get a business loan from a bank (obviously some people do), but I have met a lot of successful small business owners and not a single one of them did!

## A word on cash flow

You will soon discover that cash flow is the heartbeat of your business, and business owners usually underestimate just how much they are going to need. You will pay dearly if you get this wrong. A lot of companies go bust as a result (our first company did, as I'll share later in this book), or you could easily lose **ownership** and **control** (there are those words again) of your business.

> Majority shareholders with a cash flow problem can soon find themselves relegated to being minority shareholders or even employees of the company they founded.

# Charge what you are worth

This is a big one.

Still on the topic of money, one of the greatest dilemmas for most new business owners, particularly those in the professional services industry, is how much to charge for services. More often than not they undercharge. That is usually because they have not developed a sense of the value their services add to the lives of their customers. Let me share my experience here.

When I started my legal consultancy I honestly had no idea how much I should be charging. Besides, I was still employed, so I was really grateful for anything extra that was coming in through the business.

One day, a friend of mine, a tax consultant who had recently set up his own company, referred a client who needed assistance with drafting a staff handbook, policies and procedures to me. I did the work, sent off my invoice, which the client paid promptly and everyone was happy.

A few weeks later I got a call from my friend, who asked what I had done for the referral he had sent my way. I told him, but realised he sounded a bit perplexed, so I asked him what the matter was. Was the client unhappy with my work? On the contrary, he assured me, the client was **very** happy. The conversation then went something like this.

'So what's the matter?' I asked.

'Nothing,' he assured me. 'How much did you charge him?'

'My usual hourly rate,' I said.

'Which is…?

'£30 an hour.' (Which, to me, seemed like a lot.)

'What?' he screamed. 'How can you charge £30 an hour for what you do? Triple it!'

Now it was my turn to scream. '£90 an hour? Are you crazy? Who's going to pay me that?' It seemed a ridiculous amount of money to me. Besides, the work only took me a few hours.

You see, I was focussed on the wrong thing. In my mind this was just a side business. I wasn't a qualified solicitor and it wasn't taking much of my time. What I should have concentrated on was: **what value does having proper policies and procedures in place add to a small company**?

For starters, it helps them fulfil their legal requirements, it informs both employer and employee of their legal rights and obligations within the employment relationship and, more importantly, it keeps the business out of an employment tribunal. Small businesses in particular can't afford to go to employment tribunals. The time wasted in preparing the case, the stress, the cost and potential damage to reputation are to be avoided at all costs. If I had focussed on those factors, I would have seen that I was grossly undercharging and undervaluing my services.

For the life of me, though, I couldn't bring myself to triple my fees, but my friend would not let me be. Every so often he would ring me up and ask if I'd adjusted my fees yet. In the end I got so fed up that I came up with the figure of £85 an hour. It was a **huge** psychological jump for me, but it seemed about right.

I remember the first time I went to pitch for a client after changing my fees. The client owned an independent school. After I had finished my pitch, she said she wanted to hire me and asked what my fees were. Oh my, you should have been there! The hair on the back of my neck stood up, my throat became constricted and I began to sweat and couldn't get the words out. My brain was saying £85, £85, just say £85, but I couldn't. In the end I stammered £50 an hour. She didn't blink. 'OK, that's fine,' she said and immediately got out her cheque book.

When I left her office I was filled with self-loathing and determined that that was the last time I was going to set my fees so low. When I visited the next client I gave them my new rate and they signed me up, no problem.

The lesson is this: if you provide great service, and what you do adds value to somebody else's life, you are well within your rights to charge accordingly for it. Charge what you are worth!

# CHAPTER 8

# *What kind of business structure should I have?*

It's important to choose the right business structure for you, considering your experience, characteristics, finance, resources, attributes and skills. This is because each business structure has different legal implications and 'pull' on your individual attributes and resources. Here are some of the more common ones.

## The sole trader

A sole trader owns the business exclusively but is also personally liable for any debts that are incurred. It's probably the most common form of business ownership in the UK. It requires very little paperwork to set up. All you have to do is to choose a trading name, open a business account, inform HMRC and you are in business! Here you are trading in your personal capacity, despite the use of a trading name. You are therefore personally liable for all the debt of the business and your personal assets are not shielded from potential creditors of the business.

The fact that you are a sole trader does not mean that you have to run the company alone. In other words, you can employ staff to assist with the business.

### Pros

✓   There is no complicated paperwork needed to set up a sole trader business.

✓   Since there is usually no one else to consult, you enjoy flexibility in business as decisions can be made very quickly.

✓   You can offer a closer, more personal service to clients.

✓   And, of course, all the business profits go to you.

### Cons

✓ Your personal assets can be called upon to satisfy your business debt. This is called unlimited liability.

✓ From personal experience, being a sole trader can be quite isolating. You also do a lot of the work yourself, at least initially, which often means you work very long, undefined hours that can impact negatively on your family life, particularly if you work from home.

✓ Doing most of the work yourself can also make it very difficult to schedule times for holidays because, usually, if you are not there, the business is not making money.

✓ As a sole trader you will soon find out that you have to be a 'Jack of all trades'. I soon discovered that being a great legal consultant does not make me a good bookkeeper!

# The partnership

This is where two or more people share not only the ownership of the business but the labour, buildings, skills and profit, as well as the loss. Each partner is responsible for their own tax on any profits.

Most partnerships have between 2 and 20 partners, though you can have more.

Setting up a partnership can be as easy as setting up as a sole trader, though I would advise that consideration should be given to getting a partnership agreement in place to deal with the relationship between the partners, particularly where one is investing more in terms of time or finance in the business. Unless the partners state how the profit of the business will be shared among them, it will be deemed to be shared 50–50. This may be unfair to the partner who is investing more into the business.

### Pros

✓ People in business partnerships can share skills and the workload, and it may be easier to pool resources to raise capital.

✓ You can also broaden the pool of services you can offer to customers and clients. For example, if a group of solicitors go into partnership, one may specialise in employment law, another, immigration, another, tax law. A wider group of services will attract a wider clientele.

✓ Also partners can have more leisure time because when one goes on holiday, the others are still working and so income is not affected.

### Cons

✓ Because more people need to be consulted, it's difficult to make decisions quickly. This is particularly important where 'instinct-driven' decisions are concerned.

I believe that, on certain rare occasions in every businessperson's life, there is an inner unction to grab an opportunity that does not seem to make sense to anyone other than the person concerned. These are often defining moments in the life of a business owner, and indeed in the business, and can be missed if you have to justify them to your partners, who may often not agree with the decision or direction you want to take.

✓ Partners are also 'jointly and severally liable' for each other's debts in relation to the business. What this means is that a person can bring an action against **all** the partners in the case of the fraud or default of just one of the partners, even though the others knew nothing about it!

This liability can extend beyond financial matters. If, for example, one of the doctors in a GP partnership fails to renew their medical licence (which legally disqualifies the doctor from practising medicine), but continues to treat patients and hurts or kills someone, all the partners can be sued for negligence, even if they were not aware of the lapse.

# The franchise

Franchising is in essence the hiring out or the granting of permission to other companies to sell a product under a certain company name in a particular area. The company selling the franchise is called the franchisor and the person paying for the franchise is called the franchisee.

Franchising is becoming increasingly popular in the UK, where there are currently around 900 franchise models.

The franchisee buys into the franchise by investing a certain sum of money and in return most of the equipment needed for the running of the franchise is supplied by the franchisor.

It has a far lower failure rate than other small business set-ups, probably due to the reasons we will look at below.

### Pros

✓  As a franchisee you benefit from trading under a well-known or established name, thus avoiding the uphill task of building one from scratch. You also enjoy monopoly in a particular area.

✓  You are your own boss and take most of the profits.

✓ Although the day-to-day running of the business is done by the franchisee, you are by no means alone and the franchisor provides advice, direction and training. One less cost for the franchisee!

✓ You benefit from established standards and practices that are already associated with a particular franchise brand.

***Cons***

✓ The methods and requirements set out by the franchisor may restrict innovation, as you are not free to do as you please with the business model.

✓ The time frame or duration of a franchise is usually determined by the franchisor and you may not have much say in the terms of termination.

## The bottom line

The bottom line is, whatever business structure you decide to set up, make sure you get good professional advice before you do so.

So where are we? We've talked about **why** every 21st-century employee must have different income streams and **how** to set up a small business as one such stream.

Now let's look at how you can use your job as a vehicle to get you there.

# CHAPTER 9

# *A job is a place to learn (not just earn!)*

There's no denying it, a lot of people literally **hate** their job! They often feel unappreciated, uninspired and obviously underpaid. Others dislike the long hours, feel stuck in their career or believe that they are in a dead-end job.

This feeling of having to get up to go somewhere every day to a place you hate, to sit in an office for the majority of your working day, with people you often don't like, and who don't like you, can have detrimental effects on your physical and mental health and general sense of self-worth.

Let's face it, most people put themselves through this horror of an existence because they need the money. I believe, however, that if you change your perception of the workplace from somewhere you go to **earn** to somewhere you go to **learn**, you will feel less helpless and hopeless, particularly if you understand that, used wisely, a job can be a **stepping stone** to setting up your own business. I'll give an example.

A few years ago a young man (I'll call him Ed) worked for a busy government department as a researcher. He'd been in the same position for many years and it didn't look like he was going to get promoted any time soon, so Ed had settled down into a life of clock-watching and mediocrity, which is sadly so prevalent in the workforce (but endemic in the civil service).

Out of the blue his department announced a 'restructuring' exercise. Translation: *we need to get rid of as many of you lazy gits as possible, and while we're at it, we'll get rid of everyone we don't like, anyone over 50 and anyone who has had the audacity to be ill more than once in the last few years'.*

Ed had had enough anyway. Despite being a hard worker, he'd been turned down for promotion many times over the years, so it was clear he wasn't going anywhere. He decided to take the money and run.

A few weeks later he was lying in bed contemplating his next move when he picked up a newspaper whose headline had caught his attention. It read something like 'Divorce rates highest among Black Africans in the UK'. *This couldn't be true, could it?* Being of African descent himself, and hardly knowing anyone who was divorced, he was intrigued and read further.

The article stated that not only are Black Africans in the UK the people group with the highest divorce rate, they are least likely to seek counselling or other interventions when things go wrong.

Still sceptical, he decided to do some research of his own. To his surprise, he discovered that the dismal findings were true (I don't know whether that is still the case). Having grown up in Nigeria – where the institution of marriage is held in very high esteem, and where a woman in particular is considered a 'failure' no matter her academic achievement or her career status if she doesn't sport a wedding ring on her finger soon after graduating from university – he decided to find out why African marriages were failing in the UK.

He discovered a surprising number of factors. Parents and elders play a big role in the success of marriages in Nigeria and are often consulted and asked to intervene when married couples are having problems. Because of the respect elders are given in Africa for their wisdom of life, their advice and instruction are nearly always applied without question and that advice nearly always supports the patching or smoothing over of issues in favour of the marriage continuing. Usually, such parents and elders are absent in the UK, so the couple are left to their own devices in resolving conflict.

Also, Nigeria is culturally a male-dominated environment, and married women are given a lot of respect and held in high esteem by society. In other words they tend to take their identity from their marital status, so the woman often succumbs to society pressure to stay married.

The dictates of the man are also paramount, so if a jealous husband asks his wife to give up her high-flying career under the pretext of wanting her to devote more time to the home and family, any protests from her will not be listened to, thus reducing her chances of becoming financially independent.

Then there is the big issue of money. In Nigeria, money is often used by men as a weapon to control women, even when, behind closed doors, the woman is the family breadwinner. To the outside world, any money she earns that belongs to her, really belongs to her husband. As mentioned before, the man can often use money to control his wife because he has a better job or business. In the UK, however, statistically, Black African women have better-paying jobs than men. That simple fact has thrown the power dynamics into a tailspin, and many women have seen that their improved financial status has given them greater choice. Probably for the first time, African women have been calling the shots; this is something many African men have found almost impossible to deal with.

Lastly, because the UK is a society where women's rights are recognised and upheld, Black African women have suddenly discovered that they too have power and rights. A right to ask 'Where are you going and what time will you be back?' (almost unheard of in Africa). A right to ask the man to move his lazy butt and go find a job if need be, and a right to ask him to leave the matrimonial home if he abuses or threatens her. Whoopee!

All of these are, in their own right, good things, but they have turned the table on the order of things as they have been for generations, and as a result, more marriages are crumbling under the change.

By the time Ed finished his research, he had made significant notes, which he tidied up and put in a dossier. At first he didn't know what to do with it, but then, he decided to send it off to his old boss.

A few weeks later he received a call from his ex-boss, thanking him for the report, which he had liked, by the way. He had taken the liberty of forwarding it to another government department that he thought might find it useful. He thanked Ed and put the phone down.

A couple of weeks later, Ed got a call from the other government department. The man on the end of the phone was very excited. His colleagues were amazed by the report. They had not realised that Black African marriages had so many props supporting them. Having understood the culture a bit more, they could now see why Black African couples, even those who managed to get through a counsellor's door, sat there stonily and refused to discuss their issues – it was because, culturally, for Africans, airing your dirty linen before strangers is anathema.

They had a proposition for him: would he mind going round the country carrying out training and workshops with marriage counselling groups, social workers and so on about the things he had written about? It would help them greatly in their approach when dealing with Black African couples. They would of course pay him, and if he would kindly put a costing together they would be happy to consider it.

*If he wouldn't mind?* **If he wouldn't mind?** Ed couldn't believe it!

Well, he did just that. One contract led to another, and let's just say he lived happily ever after.

The point I'm making is this. Ed thought he was in a dead-end job because he was 'just a researcher', but what Ed did not understand was that all those years had taught him to:

- develop a keen mind that delved below the surface
- read and absorb large amounts of information
- know where to seek and extract the necessary information

- develop his findings and be able to present that information in a comprehensive and coherent manner

- follow a line of argument through to a logical conclusion

- provide recommendations for improvement from his findings.

If you consider that all these vital skills eventually rescued Ed from a life of mediocrity, and made him quite wealthy, you begin to see your place of work as an environment not just to **earn**, but to **learn**. You will be amazed at the difference it will make to your attitude at work and how you see your job. What once seemed boring and mundane will suddenly be transformed into a haven of opportunities to hone your skills and improve your financial potential.

A shift in perspective can be magical!

# How to learn, not just earn, from your job

So here are some of the things you need to learn in your workplace.

## Learn good people skills

You must learn how to relate to people from all walks of life, Understand that when it comes to dealing with people, **one size does not fit all**.

You should learn to relate to people outside your own people group, those of a different ethnic group or sexual orientation, irrespective of how you may feel about them.

Many years ago, I worked as a Benefits Adviser in another seemingly dead-end job in the Benefits Agency (or DSS as it was then called), but from which I learned excellent people skills. Most of my colleagues didn't want to work on the front line, for good reason, but I felt it was the only place I could work if I didn't want to die from sheer boredom.

People from all walks of life came through those doors: down-and-outs, local drunks, those who had never been unemployed before and were ashamed to be there, those who had never had a job in their life and had no intention of ever getting one.

I learned to deal professionally, respectfully and sympathetically with people who were often frustrated, irate, vulnerable, depressed and sometimes downright dangerous (I had a loaded gun pointed at me once), but after working in that environment, I can deal with anyone.

## Learn transferable skills

Transferable skills are skills that are needed in any industry, such as IT skills. You should at least have a good working knowledge of Microsoft® Office programs such as Word and Excel, basic numeracy skills, decision-making skills, the ability to work to deadlines, good organising skills and the ability to use your initiative.

Many of these skills are now classified as 'soft skills' in that they are not necessarily obtained through formal education but can be acquired from any sphere of life, such as volunteering, previous jobs, sport, home life or hobbies. They are imperative in the workplace and are increasingly what prospective employers are looking for.

# Learn formally

Get as much training as possible, particularly in any area you have identified that you want to set up a business in. Get it now while someone else is paying for it. Once you have your own business, all training expenses are coming out of your profit, so get as much as you can now.

# Learn to socialise

Some people are just so stand-offish. Would it really kill you to join the others for a drink at the local pub for an hour after work?

'But they always get so rowdy and usually end up drunk. It's just not me,' you say.

Well, if that's the case, order a soft drink when they order a whisky. It's not what you drink that matters; it's about presence and participation.

The sad fact is that most decisions on promotion are made in the pub, not in the interview room. So do yourself a favour!

# Learn to put yourself forward for responsibility

Too many people hide at work. They just want to do their little bit, interact as little as possible and go their merry way at the end of the day. (Much as I did, but I found it was counterproductive).

I am often reminded about one of my old bosses who benefitted greatly from applying this principle. At the time, the company I worked for was facing some financial challenges so it began to look for ways to raise capital.

Fortunately, one of the assets was a massive six-storey building in the middle of a very lucrative part of London, which was barely being used. However, to make it attractive to potential tenants, it needed major restructuring and refurbishment, and nobody wanted the hassle of undertaking it. But my boss was very smart! She could smell an opportunity. So she put herself forward to oversee the project. The whole thing probably took about six months, and it happened at the beginning of the whole 'project management' phenomenon.

The minute she finished she started looking for a new job and, because she put that project on her CV, prospective employers were fighting over her. I am told the next job she got almost doubled her salary; and she was already on very good money.

## Learn to keep your eyes open!

Watch how things are done within your company and start thinking of how it could be done better and more efficiently. If you were the CEO of the company you work for, what would you change and why? Make notes and start strategizing. You will be amazed at what will come out of your observations.

## Learn excellent presentation skills

It is a fact that people with good public speaking skills:

✓ get promoted quicker

✓ command the respect of colleagues and customers alike

✓ are able to influence people into buying goods and services and are therefore considered an asset by their employers.

I can remember a job I did once where there seemed to be an unspoken (but no less real) belief among my colleagues that black people on my level had got the job because of their colour; in other words as an act of tokenism. I was determined to disabuse them of that impression! I knew I had got the job because, as my boss (who was one of the interviewers) later told me, I was the best candidate by far out of eight interviewees.

But how could I get others to see that? I devised a plan: every time we had a staff meeting with all the managerial bigwigs, I would stand up and say something. It might be to ask an (intelligent) question, or give an opinion or counter-opinion on something that had been said. Anything that would let them know that I had a brain in my head.

The minute I began to do this, my colleagues' attitudes towards me changed. First of all, I got noticed. Secondly, my boss began to pass more strategic work to me that made my job a lot more interesting. I would often be asked at meetings if I had anything to say on a topic being discussed. In other words, my opinion began to carry weight and was valued. Something strange that I had not anticipated also occurred.

My colleagues would consult me when they were having problems knowing how to apply the law in different client scenarios. In other words, I became the go-to person if you needed legal advice.

I remember when I resigned. They bought me one of those 'Sorry to see you go' cards. It was interesting the number of people who mentioned that staff meetings were going to go back to being so boring now, and that the only time they hadn't fallen asleep during a staff meeting was when I was in attendance.

Good public speaking skills get you noticed because, when you are able to express yourself clearly, confidently and convincingly in public, people equate that to intelligence, and that can't hurt.

Look for opportunities to hone your skills in this area. Offer to do a presentation on what your job entails at the next staff meeting. It just might save your job. Maybe even your boss doesn't know it and might realise how vital your role actually is to the company when the next redundancy exercise comes around!

## Learn to manage your time and prioritise

As I said before, time management is one of the greatest problems for the small business owner. Time is your greatest asset, and you seem to have less of it when you are self-employed! This is particularly the case in the early days of your business when you will probably be doing nearly everything by yourself.

While you are still in your job, I would encourage you to organise your priorities daily, ideally at the start of your day. Here's a suggestion: make three columns under the headings **Urgent**, **Important**, **Can wait** and insert all your tasks for the day under those three columns. Next, allocate a projected time to each task. It will help you stay focussed and help you weed out time-wasting activities. Mixing those three things up can cost you dearly. Ask any business owner who has ever missed a tax return deadline!

# Every job has something to teach you

One of the 'worst' jobs I have ever done is telemarketing research, where you ring up and disturb people who, after a hard day at work, have just sat down to dinner, only to have you ask them a list of annoying questions about things they care nothing about!

Most of my colleagues hated it, and it paid very badly. But I learned many skills from that job. I learned about great customer service from the questions in the surveys. I learned excellent negotiating skills and not to take no for an answer. (It's no easy feat to get people to give up their time to answer questions about something they couldn't care less about.) I learned to keep statistics and record information correctly. I learned how to use leading and open-ended questions.

In fact, I put everything I learned on that job into a training package on customer service called 'How to find and keep your customers', which companies now pay me good money to deliver. So there!

# CHAPTER 10

# *Making the transition*

Earlier on I spoke about working at the Benefits Agency.

One day I was sitting at my desk with about half a dozen of my colleagues and somebody referred to an incident that had happened at work about 10 years earlier.

I was amazed. 'How long have you been here, then?' I asked. 'About 12 years,' she replied.

I couldn't believe it: 12 years in the same job and she was still at the bottom of the heap with no chance of promotion. I asked other colleagues the same question. All of them came back with similar responses; some had even been there longer. It seemed I had been there the least time: six years, and, in between, I had taken a three-year study break to get a degree in law.

My manager waded in on the conversation. She too had been there for over 10 years. I knew she wasn't happy there. 'Why did you stay?' I asked her. 'Well, at least I have a job,' she promptly replied.

I had recently gotten married. When I arrived home that night, I announced to my husband that I was going to resign.

'Why?' he exclaimed, duly concerned.

I told him about our conversation in the office. 'I don't want to turn into them,' I said. Obviously he wasn't happy and tried to talk me out of it, but I was adamant. The next day I went in and tendered my resignation. But I paid a huge price for my impulsiveness because I didn't get a job for the next six months! So, I wouldn't advocate that kind of emotion-driven, rash decision-making to anyone.

# Look before you leap

One of the reasons people stay in a job they would rather leave is because they are scared of the financial unknown if they resign. How will they pay their bills before the business takes off? More importantly, how will they survive?

I would definitely not advise you to make the type of foolish, rash decision I did and suddenly give up your job to start a business. Besides, I was able to do it then because we didn't have any children yet, and I was probably influenced by the arrogance of youth.

But there's nothing that says there can't be a transition period. When I decided to start my business, following my eureka experience that I spoke of in the introduction, being older, wiser and financially responsible for two kids, I didn't repeat my earlier mistake of going in the next day and handing in my resignation.

First of all I researched how much money I would need to set the business up. Since I was setting up a business I believed I could initially run from home, my overheads were low and my initial expenditure was limited to things such as stationery, a computer, printer and business cards, all of which I discovered I could do with about £1,000.

I had read that most businesses take about two years to turn a profit, so I didn't initially plan to leave my job within the first two years. As it happened, within a year my business income was matching my salary, and within two years it was doubling it. My son's autism diagnosis forced the situation and I had to leave my job to take care of him, anyway, but by then my business was already making money.

A few years later my husband (who was an in-house solicitor for a medical firm at the time) decided that he wanted to set up his own law firm. Once again we were armed with the knowledge that the business would need at least two years before we would start turning a profit. Also, setting up a law firm requires a lot more financial input than some other businesses. There was the office, the IT system, the phone system, staffing costs, professional fees, and so on. My husband asked if it was possible for me to handle the bills from my income for the first two years if need be.

This required major financial restructuring.

The first thing I did was go out and buy the boys enough clothes to last them over the next two years. *My boys may have to go hungry for the next two years,* I thought, *but by God they will be stylish!*

I then sat down and looked at our outgoings. Where could savings be made? What could we live without? Eating out, holidays and other luxuries all had to go. I cut our family budget down to the barest minimum. Lidl replaced Sainsbury's for the monthly shopping. All service providers were examined and, if I could get it done cheaper elsewhere, I switched. All the savings I made went into a separate pot.

That experience taught me two vital lessons:

1.  You can actually live on a lot less than you think.

2.  If you want something badly enough, you will find a way to make it happen.

> My boys may have to go hungry for the next two years, but by God they will be stylish!

# Do your homework!

Starting a business can be an exhilarating experience, but it can also put a huge strain on your family, particularly if they have not bought into your vision and what you are trying to achieve.

I am a strong supporter of the life philosophy of the late Mary Kay Ash, the founder of the billion-dollar cosmetics company Mary Kay:

### God first, then family, then business.

If you do not get your family's support very early on, it can have devastating effects on your business and your life in general. Many marriages break up as a result of a business start-up. **Think about that for a second:** something that should have been of great benefit to your family ends up being the reason for a split.

When you decide to go into business, I encourage you to have a sit-down with your spouse and your children (if you have them). It is important that they all understand what you are trying to achieve and why you are trying to achieve it. More importantly, they must be made aware of their role in it and the sacrifices they are going to have to make in order for you to succeed. You may no longer be able to pick them up from school every afternoon and you are definitely going to miss a few sports matches and school plays!

It is also important that you reassure them that you love them and that they are number one in your life. As much as possible, let them know how things are going with the business along the way, so they understand those times when they rush to jump into your arms and you gently push them away, or snap at them and retreat to your bedroom (times that should be kept to a minimum, by the way). They need to realise that it's not because you don't love them, but that you are just under a lot of stress because you didn't have enough cash to pay salaries this month, again.

It's at times like this that a spouse, or a close friend, can be a great ally as they may know how to explain to a hurt and crying child that the other parent still loves them but is just having some problems at work at the moment and will take them to the fair at the weekend to make up for it.

Sometimes entrepreneurs also need reigning in and reminding of what is **really** important. Spouses are great at reminding us! Don't make the common mistake of thinking that providing increased financial benefits (the expensive holidays, the new car) substitute for your presence and participation in the home. The sad truth is that very few of us get the balance right, but we must be seen to be trying to. The success of the business should make you grow as a family, not grow apart.

So that's it, guys. That should be more than enough to get you started. Now let me give you some tips to make sure you succeed.

# CHAPTER 11

# *15 tips for running a successful business*

# Tip 1. Develop the '3 Ps' – Person, Process and Product

## Person

Successful entrepreneurs have certain character traits that you must develop if you want to succeed in business.

One of them is the ability to work hard. If you are currently employed and you think you work too hard, when you start to work for yourself you will work 10 times harder! Running a business and being lazy just do not go together.

If you also have a tendency to procrastinate, you need to deal with that. I define procrastination as waiting to do next week what you should have done last month.

A lot of businesses (particularly professional services) require strict deadlines, and non-adherence to those deadlines can cost you dearly. For instance, not filing your income tax return with HMRC on time attracts a monetary fine (which increases the greater the delay). Bottom line: learn how to manage your time and prioritise.

You also need to learn to multitask. When you are employed, you are pretty much spoon-fed. If your wage slip is late, you pop down to the accounts department and they chase it for you. If your computer screen suddenly goes blank, you pick up the phone and call IT support and they sort it out for you. When you are self-employed, particularly in the beginning, you have to wear a lot of hats, but don't be put off.

When you start a business, money may be tight. It is not unusual for you to be unable to draw a salary from the business for a considerable amount of time, or at least until things stabilise, so you must be disciplined with whatever money you have.

You must also be disciplined in the way you work. Do what needs to be done when it needs to be done.

Keep investing in yourself. Stay abreast of changes and developments in your industry. Keep attending seminars, reading books, doing anything and everything that will improve your game.

# Process

The Process is anything that the business needs in order to succeed. It can include your IT system, your phone system, your staff policies and procedures, and so on.

One important thing to note is that, very early on, you must put systems in place to ensure that your business is not dependent on you. If your business is dependent on your physical presence in an office for it to succeed or for money to come in, I would suggest that you have not created a business, you have created a job – the very thing that you were probably trying to escape from when you started the business in the first place!

Determine from the start to create a working environment that makes people feel valued – a place that **you** would want to get up in the morning to go to – and **treat your staff well!** Most people who leave to go to another job don't do it just for the money; they want to feel appreciated and know that their contribution matters.

Make sure you have all your staff contracts, policies and procedures in place, and that staff familiarise themselves with them early on. Also, set up clear channels for discussing and resolving any issues of concern to staff. From my experience, businesses that do these things have fewer disgruntled employees and a more productive workforce.

Give praise often and reward your staff. Rewards don't always have to be monetary in nature. Something as simple as buying everyone ice creams on a hot summer's day shows that you care about them, or giving them an extra half hour for lunch on a warm day so they can sit in the park goes a long way.

When you are starting out and hiring staff, you need to hire those who are hungry for a new adventure, those who are clearly talented and those who can identify and nurture the talent in others.

You can hire people who are just starting out and therefore need to grow in the job for entry-level positions, but not at strategic level. For higher positions you need people who know what they are doing and can take decisions in your stead, and who don't require close monitoring or hand-holding.

> If your business is dependent on your physical presence in an office for it to succeed or for money to come in, I would suggest that you have not created a business, you have created a job – the very thing that you were probably trying to escape from when you started the business in the first place.

As soon as possible, start delegating mundane and time-draining activities to your staff. I find that, if you are not careful, administrative tasks can swallow up your time and energy, when you need to stay uncluttered to provide strategic direction for the business.

No matter how great your business vision is, if you don't have the right people in place to execute the vision, knowingly or unknowingly, your staff will sabotage it. Hire people who are skilled, passionate and believe in what you are trying to achieve. Particularly as a small business, it is important that your staff understand and are frequently reminded of your vision, and that they are inspired by it. Inspiration is important because inspired employees look way beyond their salary (which may not be much to write home about in the early days); they are willing to go the extra mile, work late when necessary, etc. Getting 'emotional buy-in' from your staff for your vision is one of the biggest keys to your success.

## Product

The Product is not just your physical product - although how a product is presented is crucial  - but also the way you offer the product or service, which includes things like your customer service (at which you should aim to be first class). To ensure that good customer service is successfully developed in your business, **all** staff must have an understanding of excellent customer service and **all** must play a role in achieving it.

# Tip 2. Get on a stage!

*'Knowledge is the new currency and public speaking is the new bank.'* Robert Kiyosaki

It's strange how things have turned out. The internet has changed everything - we have moved from not having enough information to information overload. What people are  looking for now is someone who can wade through the sea of information out there in relation to a particular product or industry, acquire the relevant knowledge and present it to them in a simplified way that they can understand – and they are willing to pay for it. Hopefully that is what I am doing for you with this book!

Therefore, whenever you have an opportunity to speak publicly about your product, seize it with both hands.

Speaking publicly about your services has a profound effect on your listeners.

First of all, people who speak well in public are considered more intelligent than others.

But, even beyond that, there is something almost magical about standing on a stage and speaking with confidence. In the mind of the listener it not only makes you memorable, it positions you as an expert in your field, and that's what you want. You need to be seen as the go-to person in your industry.

> Public speaking is one of our greatest fears but, when done well, the financial benefits can be enormous. I offer seminars and one-to-one coaching in this area. For further information, visit www.bebeclement.com/training.

Also, the 'rule' that people buy from those they know, like and trust is very true. When you speak well in public, people form an opinion about you, and if you come across well through what you say, your body language and topic knowledge, this should help them form the opinion that they like you. That opinion will influence them into buying whatever product you are selling from you.

Speaking from a platform also saves you a lot of time. Imagine if you had a room full of 200 people and you had to pitch to each of them individually. First of all, it would take time to set up meetings, get their contact details (that's if they are willing to give them to you) and then impress them on an individual basis. But once they've all heard you speak well, you have already jumped over many of those hurdles.

No matter your product, it can be sold from a stage. You just have to be innovative. If you are not very confident, start small.

Supposing you sell cosmetics. You could hire a venue, invite your friends and family, and do a short, interesting talk about the product, how it works and what value it can add to their lives. Your job as a speaker is not just to inform but, more pertinently, to *transform*. You must clearly convey **how** your product meets a need or solves a problem in your audience's life. Transform the audience's thinking, ideas and beliefs about whatever you are talking about and have the product for sale afterwards.

**Be innovative.**

A couple of years ago, a potential client of mine had a company that organised wedding exhibitions – you know the type where bridal gowns, flower arrangements, and everything to do with weddings will be on display. I'm a speaker and knew there would be a lot of people attending and I wanted in, but I didn't know much about weddings. I have, however, given talks on marriage, and I know that people get so caught up in the preparation for the wedding (which only lasts a day), that they forget they then have to go on and live out a marriage (for the rest of their lives). I've always believed that, if people spent a quarter of the time they spend on wedding planning preparing for the marriage, there would be far fewer divorces. Perhaps I could help them with some tips.

I asked if I could have a 10-minute slot to speak about '10 tips for a successful marriage'. The organiser wasn't so sure, but he took a gamble and agreed. I then set up a stand in the room to sell my products, CDs and DVDs of previous talks I had done (none of which were on marriage, by the way).

I spoke at the exhibition and it was a huge success. I can honestly say it was the highlight of the day. Afterwards I was swamped by people at my stand, many of whom were already married, were having problems and wanted advice. After hearing me speak, they thought I was a marriage counsellor! And, of course, I sold my products. Believe me, it's worth doing.

# Tip 3. Develop a mindset for success

There is a saying that whether someone says that they can or that they can't, they are right both times! The Bible puts it in a similar way: 'For as a man thinks in his heart, so is he' (Proverbs 23:7[1]). It is extremely important that you believe in yourself and your ability to succeed in business, because your belief system impacts upon everything you do, and indeed the way you do it.

Remember, if nobody else in your life believes you can do this, **I do!**

> Whether a person believes that they can or that they can't, they are right both times.

# Tip 4. Be a trend spotter

Good businesspeople are visionaries. They see what others do not see, or at least see it way before others do. They are less interested in what people are into now and more interested in what they will be into in five years' time. You must be that way too.

According to Wikipedia, it was while working at the NEC that Charles Dunstone, co-founder of Carphone Warehouse,

> '...first spotted the potential of mobile phones and the future of mobile communications. At that time, handsets were large, cumbersome and mainly purchased by big business and large organisations. Corporate clients were well catered for but small businesses, the self-employed and the general public had nowhere to go. Dunstone realised that mobile phones would eventually become ubiquitous and named his company the Carphone Warehouse (CPW) to serve this larger market.
>
> In July 2000 the company floated on the London Stock Exchange and, based on an issue price of 200p, the company was valued at approximately £1.7 billion.[2]

He saw what others did not see!

# Tip 5. Don't try to reinvent the wheel – improve it!

Some people feel that, in order to do well in business, they must have some fantastic new idea or innovative product. Nothing could be further from the truth. Your product can simply be an improvement or a new slant on an existing product and it will sell. Look at McDonald's. Of course, hamburgers existed before McDonald's came along but Ray Kroc, who bought the company from the McDonald brothers in 1961, introduced the ethos of consistency – that every hamburger and product sold in any McDonald's outlet should be exactly the same. It was mainly this ethos that turned McDonald's into the global phenomenon that it is today.

# Tip 6. Establish your unique selling point (USP)

Imagine if you and two other businesses were trying to sell the same product to a potential client. What would differentiate your product or make you stand out, such that a potential customer would choose your product over the others? That's your USP and that's what you must push. My USP is that I am a Black, female speaker (and there are not many of those around in the UK at the moment). Also, my talks not only help you be the best that you can be in a particular area of your life, they also arm you with the tools with which to do so.

# Tip 7. Look for new and emerging industries with low start-up costs

The 16th December 2015 edition of *Wall Street 24/7*[3] highlighted some industries that the writers considered 'dying industries'. These included newspaper and print media industries (largely due to people now preferring digital media), video and disc rental and many more.

Before you start your business, it is worth researching the area you wish to go into. There is no point in investing large amounts of money in an industry that the world is not going to need in 10 years' time!

Besides, investors are often attracted to new industries because they want to make a quick return on their investment and make an exit before everybody else wises up.

Emerging industries are often shrouded in mystery, uncertainty, ignorance and misconception of the facts. If you are able to understand a new industry quickly, you can establish yourself as the expert or go-to person in that field. Being seen as the go-to person in a particular industry is one of the greatest marketing tools of the current age.

# Tip 8. Keep your profit high and your overheads low

The internet has totally changed the way we do business. Million-pound businesses are now being run from home, so think before you go and get that swanky office overlooking the river that is going to set you back thousands of pounds, and consider whether you could in fact run your business from your kitchen table and save yourself substantial overheads.

What about that glossy brochure that is probably going to gather dust in your filing cabinet? Could your print marketing needs be served sufficiently with a well-designed, more affordable format? The point is, the less money you shell out, the more you get to keep.

# Tip 9. Go where the money is

They say a rising tide lifts all boats. There are some places where you can position your business that will almost automatically make money. Right now it's the internet. The potential of the internet for making money in business, particularly small businesses, is being realised daily. There are so many things you can do to monetise the knowledge you have in your particular area, including webinars, digital downloads, podcasts and paid online membership access to your material. Find out how the internet can work for you.

# Tip 10. Go forth and multiply!

You should look at your core business as a tree – a tree that must bear fruit. Look for ways that a single business entity can lead to other opportunities.

As you have read, one of our businesses is a magazine called *Law Digest*. It's the global premier magazine for African lawyers. We publish it three times a year. It's in its fourth year and is doing very well.

On the back of the success of this magazine we decided to hold an annual conference in Nigeria on asset recovery and international litigation. That conference is also now in its fourth year. Year on year we have increased the number of delegates attending, from the UK, America, Switzerland and other parts of Africa. The delegates pay an entrance fee (another source of income) and the conference is usually sponsored (yet another income stream).

At the conference, people are able to hire exhibition stands to showcase their products (you've guessed it – another source of income).

In 2015 we also set up the *Law Digest* Africa Awards to recognise and reward African law firms making positive contributions to the development of the legal system in their countries, and also those that are contributing positively to the growth and development of their economies. The event is a very glitzy affair. It's held in one of the best hotels in Nigeria and standard tickets start from US$100. In its first year we had over 200 delegates. Again the event attracts sponsorship. Can you see how a single business venture has given birth to a number of other lucrative income streams?

You must find innovative ways to make your business do the same.

# Tip 11. Learn how to deal with failure

Failure is part of life. Get over it! It's all part of the journey. I can assure you that there is no successful business owner who did not fail along the way. Not every business deal Richard Branson made turned to gold, and not every product Apple has made has been successful.

Steve Jobs designed a computer nicknamed 'The Cube'. Despite his prediction that it would sell 200,000 units per quarter, in the first quarter it sold less than half that, and in the second quarter less than 30,000 units. Jobs later admitted that he had overdesigned and overpriced the Cube (Isaacson, 2011)[4].

Mary Kay Ash, the founder of a global billion-dollar cosmetics company, said that 'We fail forward to success'. What she meant is that the accomplishments we have that are eventually recognised as 'success' by our peers are really a series of failures, like a baby learning to walk. The process consists of a long series of repeated fallings down. I've had many business failures along the way.

My husband and I set up our first business when we first got married, over 21 years ago. Armed with little more than the arrogance of youth, we started a company that was importing specialist pasta from Italy.

At the time, the British palate was only just exploring 'off-the-radar' types of pasta and we introduced almost unheard of varieties, such as squid ink. We added to the range items such as pistachio nuts and began supplying local independent shops. We stocked the items in our hallway because we couldn't afford storage.

In addition, we began to make hampers with our specialist products as a small side business. Slowly but steadily it began to grow.

Out of the blue one day we received an order from an airline that wanted to introduce our range as part of their menu – and they wanted a lot! We were ecstatic. The only problem was the airline wanted a 90-day turnaround, whereby we would supply them with the products (no cash down) and they had 90 days to pay us our money. It wasn't that we didn't trust them, but it meant we would have to stump up the money to order the products first and then wait to be repaid. The only problem was we didn't have any money and we didn't know anyone else who did, either!

*Not to worry,* we thought. *We would go to our local friendly bank – the one always telling us in their TV adverts how eager they are to help small businesses.* Armed with the order letter from the airline, we confidently booked an appointment with our bank manager to raise the capital.

Needless to say, they said no. We couldn't believe it.

'But why?' I asked, as we sat across the desk from the man who seemingly held our fate in his hands.

'You have no collateral,' he said. 'How will you pay it back?'

To which I retorted, 'But read the letter. We will get paid in three months and you will get your money. You can contact the client yourself. You can…'

But he wasn't convinced and nothing we could say would make him budge. Bottom line: we didn't **own** anything against which the bank felt comfortable lending.

We were so disappointed and discouraged by that experience that we stopped trading and wound down the company altogether!

Since then we have gone on to found other businesses that have been very successful. Failure in business can be painful, but it is never fatal (even bankruptcy doesn't last forever). The important thing you need to do is learn lessons from your failure:

✓ What **exactly** failed in the process?
✓ Why did it fail?
✓ What could I have done differently?
✓ What have I learned from this experience?
✓ What do I need to do to stop it happening again?

Finding answers to those questions will ensure that you don't give up but get right back up and try again. Just like we did.

# Tip 12. Deal with bad habits

Let's just get it out there. Many of us are just plain lazy. We often know what is needed to get us to the place of success in our lives, but lack the motivation and fortitude to follow through on what we know. If you are lazy, it is unlikely you will do well in business, because being an entrepreneur is hard work. Very hard work.

Procrastination is another thing that will stop you doing well in business. Remember, my definition of procrastination is leaving till next week what you should have done last month.

A lot of things in business are time-sensitive, and if you do not have the discipline of doing what should be done, when it should be done, you will miss out on many opportunities, which sadly may never come round again. Which leads me to something else:

# Tip 13. Trust your instincts

I enjoy reading biographies of successful people, particularly successful entrepreneurs, and one of the things they all have in common is that, at pivotal times in their lives, they listened to their instincts, and that single act of courage led to or played a large role in their success.

At some point in your business life you will feel an inner push. An unspoken command to **jump. Now.** Often when that happens it doesn't make sense to us (nor usually to others). The timing may not seem right, the market may be in downturn, and the situation may be screaming *hold your fire!* but may I implore you, once you receive that inner nudge, to **respond**. Don't try to rationalise it, because conventional wisdom often kills initiative. For many, those moments come once in a lifetime and can make all the difference between success and failure. Don't let fear of the unknown keep you bound to mediocrity and the familiar.

# Tip 14. Find your *why*

At the start of this book, I highlighted the reasons why it is imperative that the 21st-century employee develops different income streams. The **whys** I gave are applicable to all employees, but you must find your own **why**, something personal to you that will continue to motivate you to find a way over the hurdles, pick yourself up after yet another door has been slammed in your face, and try again and again after you have faced failure and defeat. In other words, all the things you will face in your quest for financial freedom.

When my first child was aged two he was diagnosed as being severely autistic. As he became older, his diagnosis broadened to include ADHD, dyspraxia, speech and language delay, and significant learning disabilities.

As a Christian I am full of faith and hope regarding his future, but the fact is we do not know if he will be able to hold down a job or provide for himself financially. He is my **why**. It is important to me and my husband that we go to our graves knowing we have done all we can do to make financial provision for him and his brother.

I have other **whys** that are not as personal.

I believe we are supposed to use our wealth to lift people up along the way, so my **why** includes the charities I support in the United Kingdom and in Africa.

I also believe we are to leave a legacy, put our footprint on the world or, as Beyoncé said in her song, let the world know 'I was here'. One of the best ways to do that is to build a business that outlives me and serves generations to come.

Your **why** can be anything. I recently met an aspiring business owner who confided that his **why** is to prove wrong the person who told him, in the early days of establishing his business, that he would never make it.

It may be that ex-husband who said you would never amount to anything, or even to quieten your own voice in your head telling you that you can't do it. It doesn't matter what your **why** is – just find it.

# Tip 15. Take risks!

I read some research carried out a few years ago among a group of elderly people. They were asked to name their top five regrets.

'I should have taken more risks' ranked in the top three nearly every time.

Financial success, like success of any kind, is always intentional. You must commit to doing well in business. There are very few success stories of those who merely dipped their toe in the water in any sphere of life.

One the saddest stories I ever read was in the biography of one of my heroes, Steve Jobs (Isaacson, 2011[5]), about a friend of his, Ron Wayne, whom Jobs approached to adjudicate between him and Steve Wozniak, and in particular convince Wozniak to let Apple own his circuits and computer designs, which he finally agreed to do.

In gratitude, Jobs offered Wayne a 10% stake in the new partnership that was formed as a result. Wayne originally agreed, but then developed cold feet and withdrew from the partnership. He was afraid that, because the company had been set up as a simple partnership rather than as a corporation, the directors would be personally liable if it went belly up, and he didn't want to take that risk.

If he had stayed on, at the end of 2010 he would have been worth $2.66 billion dollars! Instead, he was then living alone in a small home in Nevada on welfare.

Need I say more? **Take risks!**

# CONCLUSION

## Be a 'man of Issachar'.

In the Bible there are a group of men spoken about in revered tones. They are called the men of Issachar and the Bible says these men *'Understood the times, and knew what Israel should do'*[1] (1 Chronicles 12:32)[1].

I think that in order to do well in these times, you must become a 'man, (or woman), of Issachar'.

# Understand the times

My generation belongs to the industrial age. The industrial age, like every age before it, required certain skills and professions to thrive.

When the British went to colonise Africa, they steered would-be educated Africans towards professions that would feed the industrial age and ensure its survival. These fields included accountancy, law, medicine, engineering, administration and the like.

During the industrial age, the workplace was set up in such a way that most employees started a career with a 'job for life' mindset. They spent years climbing the corporate ladder, being promoted every few years, and looking forward to their retirement party, where the boss would sum up years of near slavery on their part in a few nice words and present them with a gold watch, after which they would slink off into the night of retirement, boat cruises and pottering around in the garden.

Dear reader, **we are no longer in the industrial age!** The day of the job for life is gone, and thankfully, I can now buy my own gold watch, thank you very much.

Like the men of Issachar, it is imperative that you recognise the times.

We are now in the **information or digital age.** A different set of skills, knowledge and education is needed to thrive in these times. Even the psychology of the age is different. Whereas 20 years ago staying in the same job for 15 or 20 years would have been viewed as a sign of stability by a prospective employer, today it could be considered a sign of laziness or a lack of ambition!

# Knowing what to do

The key to thriving in this new era is knowing how to respond to this change. As a 21st-century employee, you must be savvy. You can stay employed, but must ensure that you develop different income streams in case your employment should end for any reason.

You must also develop new skills. There is increasingly less emphasis on paper qualifications in this new era. More important is how you can articulate what you know and present it in a format that makes a **connection** with clients, colleagues and potential employers. As a result, one of the most essential skills of this new era (if not **the** most important) is the ability to communicate clearly, confidently and convincingly, particularly in public. Increasingly we are being asked to 'present' in our line of duty, and those who can do so well, can expect to be promoted faster than their colleagues, gain more respect from colleagues and clients and 'sell' more.

# Patience is not a virtue; it's a strategy

Building wealth and becoming financially free takes hard work, tenacity, perseverance, sacrifice and time. I hope you can give all that. If not you may be better off staying in your 9-5, because as an entrepreneur you will be required to give all that and more.

But for those of you who are hungry – I mean **really hungry** and determined not to be a wage slave –I encourage you to roll up your sleeves and jump in. The stakes are high but the rewards higher.

**Good luck!**

# REFERENCES

Chapter 1

1. Hall, Rich, "Late night with Conan O'Brien", Monday, July 17,1995
2. Hendy, Paul, *The Guardian*, 9th December, 2007
3. Delgado Martin & Bunyan, Nigel, *'First flooded, then fleeced'*, Mail Online, 2, January, 2016, pg. 11
4. Ibid: pg. 12
5. Harman: *Four Maids Ltd v Dudley Marshall Properties Ltd* ([1957] Ch. 317)

Chapter 6

1. Bosma, N. and R. Harding (2007), *Global Entrepreneurship Monitor Studies*

Chapter 7

1. eMarketer, 2002
2. Isaacson, Walter, *Steve Jobs, Little Brown Book Group,* October 24, 2011,

Chapter 10

1. Ash, Mary Kay: *Mary Kay Ash - The story of America's most dynamic business woman,* 28th of June 1984.

Chapter 11

1. Holy Bible, New International version ®, NIV® Copyright ©1973, 1978, 1984, 2011 by Biblica, Inc.® Used by permission. All rights reserved worldwide- Proverbs 23:7

2.  Wikipedia, https://en.wikipedia.org/wiki/Charles_Dunstone

3.  Conner Evan and Stebbins Samuel, *America's 25 dying industries,* Wall street, 24/7, 16th of December, 2015. 2.43pm edition. Retrieved from  http://247wallst.com/special-report/2015/12/16/25-dying-industries/

4.  Isaacson, Walter, *Steve Jobs, Little Brown Book Group,* October 24, 2011,  pg. 237

5.  Ibid, pp. 65,66

Conclusion

1.  Chronicles 12:32 Holy Bible, New International Version®, NIV® Copyright ©1973, 1978, 1984, 2011 by Biblica, Inc.® Used by permission. All rights reserved worldwide

# WHAT'S NEXT FOR YOU?

Thank you for purchasing this book. I hope you will find it a vital tool to which you can refer again and again in your journey to entrepreneurship and financial freedom.

**Please connect with me...**

I believe I can continue to assist you on your journey, so, please connect with me via the following channels:

**Facebook**: fb.me/bebeclement

**Website**: www.bebeclement.com/contact

Once you connect with me I will send you tips and useful strategies to help you develop and flourish. I will also keep you updated of any future speaking events I will be attending.

Here are some special offers to assist you:

1. For 30 minutes free legal advice for any aspect of your business, contact Augustine Clement Solicitors on 0203 223 0800 quoting BC/E2E/16 to book an appointment
2. For 30 minutes free business start-up advice, enter your details at www.bebeclement.com/contact.
3. To Purchase my 6 part DVD , *'How to create, grow & protect your wealth'* for the special price of £45, visit www.bebeclement/shop and enter code ET1

Finally, I would be very grateful if you would leave a review for my book on Amazon.

Here's to your success.

*Put your signature on life!*

## Bebe

# RECOMMENDED READING

1. *Mary Kay*- By Mary Kay Ash- Harper Perenniel- 3rd edition
2. *How to get rich*- Felix Dennis- Ebury Press, 2007
3. *Reposition Yourself*- T.D. Jakes- Pocket Books, 2009

# USEFUL LINKS

1. Finance & Support - https://www.gov.uk/business-finance-support-finder
2. Set up a business - https://www.gov.uk/set-up-business
3. Small business grants - http://entrepreneurhandbook.co.uk/grants-loans/
4. Sage free business advice. http://www.sage.co.uk/business-advice
5. Federation of small businesses - www.fsb.org.uk/